THE INDEPENDEN

HONG KONC ⌐ ⌐ ⌐ ⌐

by

Colin A. Rampton

For my wife Hilary whose enthusiasm led us here all those years ago.

Edited by Giovanni Costa

Table of Contents

Introduction

The Pearl of the Orient, the City where East meets West, the World City, the City of Life - these are just some of the alternative names for the fascinating place that is Hong Kong. But calling Hong Kong a city is a little confusing – for it often refers to the business district around Central (formerly Victoria) which was the old capital of Hong Kong Island. Hong Kong is fact more than a city. Officially it's a 'territory', and before 1997 it was a British 'colony.'

There is so much more to Hong Kong than the concrete jungle which people conjure up in their minds before they arrive. Yes, there are some very densely populated areas. Indeed parts of Kowloon are amongst the most densely populated in the world. There are more than enough skyscrapers in Central, Wanchai and Causeway Bay to make your neck ache, but there are also pleasant beaches, rugged hill walks, wild animals and even farms and meadows if you are prepared to wander off the beaten track.

This travel guide will give you an insight into some of the famous attractions to be found here, as well as some less well known gems. With all considerations, it is an amazing place with many aspects which will both surprise and delight you.

Hong Kong is a hilly to mountainous territory of some 1104 km^2 (426 mi^2), situated at the south eastern tip of China, abutting the South China Sea. The highest point is Tai Mo Shan at 957 meters (3139 feet). The territory comprises

Hong Kong Island, Kowloon and the New Territories and includes some 262 outlying islands, some of which are uninhabited. There are 733 kilometers of coastline (455 miles) and there is a boundary with Mainland China.

Hong Kong is now an official Special Administrative Region (SAR) of China, having been returned from British rule during the historic handover of July 1st 1997. The slogan coined by the Chinese Communist Government at the time was 'One Country Two Systems' with the promise that Hong Kong would retain a large degree of autonomy and independence from China for the forthcoming fifty years.

The promise has largely been kept and the territory maintains its own system of law and order and government - the Legislative Council (LegCo). However, the leader of the government - the Chief Executive - is not elected by the local people but by a limited number of delegates approved by Beijing. This a bone of contention amongst some local people. On a day to day basis though, Hongkongers enjoy far more freedom and independence than their cousins in the mother country - just a few miles away.

In the pages that follow we will look at some of the background information which has made Hong Kong a unique and memorable place. We will examine some of the customs of the fascinating people who call it home and look at a selection of those destinations which the discerning traveler will not want to miss.

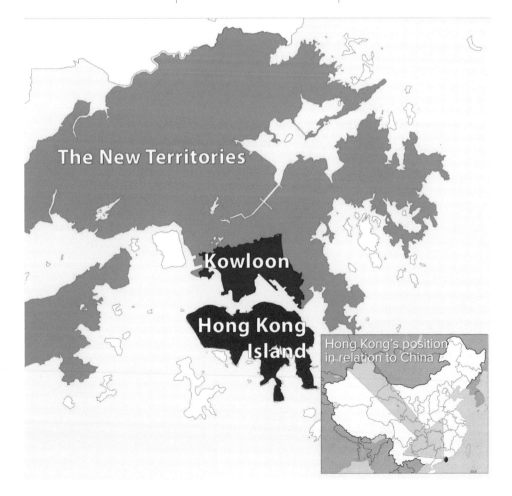

The New Territories

Kowloon

Hong Kong Island

Hong Kong's position in relation to China

Hong Kong: A Brief History

In order to understand Hong Kong today, including its people and its customs, we shall first take a look at the area's past including its time under British rule.

Early Days

Hong Kong was named in Cantonese as *heung keung* – 'Fragrant Harbor'. There are several theories about the origin of the name but the most popular is that in ancient times, sweet smelling fragrant joss sticks were made in the area and traded from the natural deep water harbor.

Archaeological evidence suggests that the region was inhabited as long ago at 5000 BCE. There is clear evidence of people with a strong Chinese influence living in the area from the Han period of the first and second centuries.

There is a theory that Hong Kong was a British creation but certainly there was a successful, if fragmented community long before the British arrived. When Hong Kong became part of the British Empire in 1841, there were about 700 villages in the area that were to become the New Territories. On Hong Kong Island itself, there were about 4000 inhabitants on land and approximately 2000 fisher folk living on and working from their boats.

British Trade with China

In the early 19th Century the British had a strong desire for Chinese goods – especially silk, tea, paper, porcelain and spices. The problem was that the Chinese had little interest in commodities that the British could offer in return. That was before the advent of opium – which was grown in British Bengal.

At first the Chinese need for opium was purely medicinal – it was in great demand for reducing pain. It soon became established however as a method of inducing pleasure and euphoria and was suddenly a very desirable commodity.

The Chinese government became very concerned about the increasing number of opium addicts and took steps to limit and later curtail the supply. This led to the First Opium War (1839-42) and the ceding of Hong Kong Island to the British.

The British naval hierarchy had espied the land and saw its great potential as an easily accessed deep water harbor, in a perfect location for trade within and beyond the South China Sea.

The Beginning of British Rule

The British flag was raised over Hong Kong Island on January 26th 1841 and, apart from a period of three and half years under Japanese occupation during World War II, the territory remained British until the handover ceremony on July 1st 1997.

A Hong Kong seal was added to the blue ensign to give the territory its own flag.

In 1959 Hong Kong was given its own coat of arms encompassing a British lion and Chinese dragon either side of a shield depicting two junks in full sail. This was added to the ensign and became the official Hong Kong flag from 1959 until the handover.

In the early days, the British quickly organized themselves. A police force was set up and roads were built. The population of the island increased in the first seven years from 7,000 to 24,000 and by 1862 it stood at 123,000.

Many Chinese workers from neighboring Guangdong Province were attracted by work opportunities and the more resourceful of the migrants learned English and took advantage of improved educational opportunities for their children.

The Expansion of the New Colony

The Kowloon peninsula, just across the harbor was also allocated to Britain to give them more land under the 1860 Convention of Peking.

Present day Kowloon is very densely populated and it is hard to imagine that in the early days it was largely undeveloped and used mainly by the Colonials for tiger hunting expeditions!

The leasing of the New Territories for a 99 year period from China in 1898, was arranged essentially to obtain farmland to help feed the speedily growing population.

The addition of the New Territories increased the land area eightfold and added another 100,000 to the population.

It was in 1984 as the expiry of this historic lease was on the horizon, that the famous 'Joint Declaration' was signed by Chinese Premier Deng Xiaoping and UK Prime Minister Margaret Thatcher.

This was the deal which enabled the whole territory to be returned to China, on the basis that it would be impractical to split it up.

Early Development

From its early days Hong Kong's position in the South China Sea allowed it to develop into an 'entrepot'. This is a port where goods are stored in transit from one part of the world to another. Shipping became increasingly important to the colony's economy.

Today the docks at Kwai Chung boast one of the largest container terminals in the world.

Apart from the Japanese occupation period, Hong Kong has always enjoyed the status of a free port where goods could be traded without restriction and fortunes made by hard work.

Colonial civil servants and private businessmen arrived from Britain and with an abundance of local Chinese laborers ('coolies'), ambitious building and development projects soon got under way.

The 'coolies' quickly gained a reputation for uncomplaining hard work. Although their working conditions were poor by modern standards, they were still able to send money home. As the news spread of opportunities in the colony, many more came.

The colony was ruled by a succession of Governors - many of whose names can still be found in local street names - and Hong Kong became more and more successful.

Schools and universities were established and opportunities for local Chinese were gradually created so they too become a part of the success.

Hong Kong Disasters

All did not run smoothly, of course, and the colony had its fair share of disasters.

There was a tragic fire at Happy Valley racecourse in 1918. More than 600 Chinese racegoers lost their lives when a highly flammable mat-shed was consumed by fire in seconds. This led to the building of more robust shelters at the course.

The colony also suffered a direct hit by an unnamed typhoon, with a consequent tidal wave in 1937. A staggering 11,000 people lost their lives in this natural disaster.

The Shek Kip Mei fire of 1953 destroyed a shanty town of 53,000 mainland immigrants living in squalor on a Kowloon hillside. But the tragedy directly led to a huge government investment in the provision of public housing for those affected, and for other people living in 'squatter villages.'

The Japanese Occupation

The darkest period of Hong Kong's history began on Christmas Day 1941 when, after 18 days of fierce fighting, the colony surrendered to overwhelming Japanese forces who had invaded from the North across the Chinese border.

The Governor and other major government officials were interred in prison camps for the duration of the war.

Three years and eight months of hard, often brutal occupation began under Japanese Imperial rule. There were inadequate food supplies for local people and items such as rice, oil, flour, salt and sugar were strictly rationed. Many people did not have enough to eat and died of starvation.

Stories emerged later of atrocities committed by the occupying troops against the locals, and during the course of the occupation an estimated 10,000 civilians were killed and thousands more were beaten and tortured.

The withdrawal ended after Japan surrendered following the dropping of atom bombs on Nagasaki and Hiroshima.

The British returned and people tried to get on with their lives. The resilience of Hongkongers was demonstrated in the way they coped in the months following the war.

By November 1945 the economy had recovered sufficiently for free markets to be opened again.

The war had changed attitudes, however, and discriminatory rules previously practiced against the Chinese (prevention from joining social clubs, banned from certain beaches, not being allowed to live on the exclusive Peak) were abandoned. More educational opportunities became available and many Chinese students became very successful in the schools and universities.

Manufacturing and Development

During the years immediately following the war Hong Kong became a magnet for local entrepreneurs, and with their commendable work-ethic, fortunes were able to be made. Industrialization really took off in the 1950s and large numbers of goods were manufactured, mainly for export. Light industries thrived and inexpensive toys and household items were sent around the world.

Li Ka Shing was early an immigrant from China. At the age of 15, he worked for 16 hours a day in a plastics factory, before starting his own business and diversifying into real estate and shipping. He is currently in the world top 20 rich list with an estimated fortune of $US 33 billion. He is a generous philanthropist and has donated to educational institutions and hospitals in Hong Kong and China, many of which bear his name.

When much of the manufacturing moved across the border to take advantage of cheaper labor, Hong Kong continued to thrive and diversify and become the international financial center that it is today.

Numerous international companies and corporations have created their Far East headquarters in the territory and have attracted talented businesspeople from around the world, taking

advantage of a thriving economy, an industrious work force and low taxes.

Hong Kong's infrastructure has continued to develop with the building of more and more housing projects, industrial premises, offices and roads.

With a shortage of land, it has utilized reclamation and has worldwide renown for its expertise in this process.

Many projects have been created and world class architects and engineers have been attracted by numerous high tech developments and generous salaries.

A huge feat of engineering was the iconic Chek Lap Kok International Airport on Lantau Island which attracted internationally reputed architects and civil engineers. It opened in 1998, replacing the old Kai Tak Airport in downtown Kowloon. It has won many awards for its unique design and the efficiency of its operation, and is considered by many to be the best airport in the world.

Another recent and outstanding example of Hong Kong building prowess is the amazing Tsing Ma suspension bridge, which you will probably pass over on your way to and from the airport.

The Tsing Ma Bridge is the ninth longest suspension bridge in the world and the longest which carries both road and rail traffic. It is part of the Lantau link which connects Kowloon to Disneyland, Tung Chung New Town and the airport.

Construction of the bridge took five years, at a cost of HK$7.8 billion. It is 1377 meters long (4518 feet) and rises 206 meters (676 feet) above the Ma Wan Channel flowing below. It is an impressive piece of architecture.

Hong Kong engineers are highly skilled and you will see numerous high-rise developments in various stages of construction. One of the surprises here, however, is the continuing use of bamboo scaffolding even on the highest of buildings. Very skilled scaffold workers tie overlapping bamboo poles with strips of strong plastic to create very strong and durable building frameworks.

Hong Kong's Culture

Hong Kong Jockey Club

The HKJC was founded in 1884 and it is one of the oldest institutions in the territory, and its most generous donor to charity. It is a non-profit making organization that has given many billions of dollars over the years to community projects and local charities. The HKJC was given a royal charter in 1959 and up until the handover it was known at The Royal Hong Kong Jockey Club. The HKJC logo is well known throughout the territory.

The club runs and controls the two horse racing tracks in Hong Kong (Happy Valley and Sha Tin) and numerous betting outlets in all major centers. There are no private betting shops in Hong Kong, the HKJC holds a government granted monopoly on betting including horse racing, the Mark Six lottery and overseas sporting events (such as English Football). There are no casinos in Hong Kong, and if you are interested in those you will have to visit neighboring Macau (60 minutes from Central by Hover Ferry).

The horse racing season begins in September and ends in early July, when the weather is at its hottest. Race days are Wednesday evenings and either Saturday or Sunday afternoon. The meetings alternate between the two tracks. Live racing is broadcast at the venue not being used, at HKJC betting outlets and on local television. The latest electronic methods of betting have been established as well as the traditional over the counter transactions.

Many Hongkongers are serious gamblers and it is common to see hordes of people congregating in and outside the HKJC outlets on race days, avidly studying the form of the horses.

Race horses in HK are superb animals and they are kept in tip top condition in air-conditioned stables. The races attract the best horses, jockeys and trainers from around the world. All HKJC employees are strictly vetted and are forbidden to bet on race days. The organization prides itself on its races being 'clean'. For a mere HK$10 you can get into the course and watch the races. What you might lose, however is another story! Races are invariably well-attended and if you do go, be prepared to cope with large crowds.

Full Membership of the Jockey Club is quite exclusive and is by nomination and election. Members can use the boxes at the tracks as well as the leisure facilities the club operates at the Sha Tin course and at the Beas River Country Club in the New Territories.

The Independent Commission against Corruption

This institution is unique to Hong Kong. It was established in 1974 at a time when the colony was experiencing massive growth and a population explosion due to the boom in the light manufacturing industries.

The taking and giving of bribes became common in everyday services, and public servants in different disciplines were implicated.

The final straw for many came after a senior expatriate policeman suddenly departed with a large amount of unexplained funds. This prompted a mass rally in Victoria Park condemning the colonial government for inactivity in allowing the situation to develop.

The Governor at the time, Sir Murray Maclehose acted by setting up the Blair-Kerr investigation and its report recommended the formation of an independent body to deal with the problem.

The ICAC came into being with a three pronged mission - law enforcement, prevention and education. With government and community support the ICAC has gone from strength to strength to make sure Hong Kong remains one of the most transparent, and least corrupt places in the world.

Politics in Hong Kong

The Legislative Council (LegCo)
The Legislative council is the body of elected representatives who enact, amend or repeal laws in the Hong Kong Special Administrative Region (HKSAR). Legislators also debate, approve or reject projects for the spending of public funds. The council also has the power to impeach the Chief Executive.

LegCo is composed of 70 members who have been elected by one of two different methods. They are equally split between geographical and functional constituencies. All eligible voters in the territory get an opportunity to elect their geographical councilor, voting in the region in which they live. Functional councilors, however represent particular groups - Medicine, Transport and so on.

The president of LegCo is elected by the 70 councilors and he/she presides over meetings, which are held on Wednesdays. The Chief Executive has a seat on LegCo but usually only attends on special occasions.

Hong Kong has a tradition of strong female legislators and their representation is proportionally more than the Mainland. Ten of the present members are women.

Meetings are held in a new, purpose built complex in Central. The old LegCo building is a short distance away, opposite the HSBC headquarters. It was used up until 2011 and is one of the most impressive of the few remaining colonial buildings.

The present LegCo councilors are comprised of 43 members representing parties who are pro-

Beijing and 27 'Pan-Democrats' who tend to be critical of the mainland Government.

The Chief Executive
The Chief Executive is not elected by everyday Hongkongers but by an electoral college of 1200 delegates who have to be approved by the People's Congress Standing Committee in Beijing.

This is a sensitive issue, which is disliked by many local people and directly led to the 'Occupy Central' protest movement of 2015 which received worldwide publicity. The protesters want every eligible voter in the territory to have a say in the next Chief Executive election.

The Chief Executive appoints an Executive Committee of advisors who are senior civil

servants. These include The Chief Secretary who is second in command (currently female), and the Financial Secretary who plans and delivers annual budgets in consultation with other Executive Committee members.

Although Hong Kong is not a democracy in the true sense of the word, the inhabitants have a lot more freedom than in other parts of China. They have the right to demonstrate, there is a free press, transparency in government dealings and a genuine respect for law and order.

But you need to experience it yourself and the rest of this chapter outlines some useful and interesting information about the territory.

Respect for Education

Significant numbers of local people can trace their ancestry back to China and many still have relatives and certainly ancestral connections there – especially in Guangdong province.

During the cultural revolution of the early fifties when intellectuals had their books burned before being sent to re-education camps, many learned people sought the sanctuary of British Hong Kong. Consequently there is an ethos of great respect for education.

Hong Kong boasts several world class universities and the general standard of education is very high in all disciplines.

Graduation at any of the universities is truly a proud occasion and all generations of the family attend the ceremony.

Hong Kong is home to some of the most accomplished scientists, mathematicians, musicians and technicians in the world.

Feng Shui

Although rather more a life philosophy than a religion, it is here worth mentioning Feng Shui (Cantonese 'wind and water').

This is the ancient philosophy of placing objects and buildings in a position that is harmonious with nature to bring about good fortune.

It originated from the ancient Chinese respect for natural life and the belief in the influence of cosmological forces.

Feng Shui experts are in great demand and make a very good living in Hong Kong. (Although since the Cultural Revolution, their activities have been frowned upon in China).

The practitioners (or 'masters' – predominantly male) are often called at the planning stage of building projects and consulted on the direction the building faces, the positioning of trees, walls, inside furniture and so on.

These experts' advice is also sought when people or companies move to new premises and they may call upon a series of complex calculations to inform you for example, to rearrange your furniture just so, in order to get the best qi (life force).

It is said that the architects altered the

position of the iconic Bank of China building following the advice of Feng Shui masters.

Other examples include the main entrance gate of Hong Kong Disneyland which was adjusted by 12 degrees and the installation and optimum positioning of the famous pair of bronze lions which reside outside the main HSBC building.

Religion

Traditional Chinese religious practices are common in Hong Kong and there are more than 600 temples - some in the middle of built up areas and others in rather less accessible locations, such as the Temple of Ten Thousand Buddhas above Sha Tin.

These are regularly visited by approximately 43 % of the local population. They are Buddhist temples with influences from Taoism and Confucianism.

The reverence and worship of ancestors is widely practiced with two public holidays (Ching Ming and Chung Yeung) dedicated to 'grave sweeping' - that is taking care of ancestors' tombs. Hong Kong also has a public holiday for Buddha's birthday.

Apart from the rituals of the temple, you are likely to see people burning paper replicas of bank notes, clothing, cars and even mobile phones in small braziers. These are for the use of departed relatives in the afterlife. There are shops which specialize in the sale of such items as well as joss sticks to be used in prayer rituals.

Hong Kong's past reliance on the sea and fishing is well represented in the temples and amongst the most popular are those dedicated to the sea goddess Tin Hau. (She even has an MTR station named after her).

Hong Kong has the largest outdoor seated Buddha in the world which attracts hundreds of thousands of visitors. The belief in good and bad luck is strong and many worshippers will attend Buddhist rituals to pray for a change of fortune, whether connected to work, family or affairs of the heart.

You will also find followers of all other major faiths in Hong Kong. It was a favored stopping off place for Christian missionaries, often on their way to more remote destinations. There are many Christian churches – both Roman Catholic and Protestant. The oldest is the historic St John's Anglican Cathedral in Central, opened in 1849. It is the only building in Hong Kong that holds the freehold to its land.

There are also seminaries in the Outlying Islands where priests from around the world come to study and meditate.

Various offshoots of Christian belief also have representation here – and there are Baptist, Congregational, Mormon, Jehovah's Witness and Evangelical churches.

Islamic mosques, Hindu Temples, Jewish Synagogues and a Sikh Temple are also in regular use. The places of worship alone reflect the diversity of the Hong Kong population.

Know Before You Go

Before we delve into Hong Kong's different neighbourhoods, its transportation system and its other particularities, we will first take more of a general look at this unique place.

Crime and Safety

Hong Kong is, by the standards of many crowded areas, generally a safe place. The local people are hard-working and law abiding and there is relatively little crime, especially involving tourists. Having said that, not everyone is honest and it is important to keep your wits about you in crowded places and to take proper care of your property.

Wan Chai, the famous red light district, has many bars and clubs where you will be encouraged to drink heavily and, if you are male, hostesses may invite you to buy a drink for them. You should check prices before you agree. There have been a few incidents where inebriated visitors have been robbed here when their defences were down. If you are going out on a drinking spree you'd be wise to take with you only what you are prepared to spend.

You should also beware of some of the electronic/camera shops in the Nathan Road / Tsim Sha Tsui district in Kowloon. Some of the proprietors will try to sell you goods at inflated prices. It is better to use those shops which display the Hong Kong Tourist Board logo (a red junk in full sail) on their entrances and be aware of what is a reasonable price to pay.

Obviously large crowds will attract a few pickpockets and you should be conscious of this when traveling on the MTR, wandering in crowded markets or attending a sporting event.

Author Note: You should never be complacent, but in twenty-six years of living in the territory I have only once had a mobile phone stolen from a clip on my belt, but have lost count of the number of times people have pointed out that I dropped some cash, that my bag was open, or that something was protruding from my pocket.

HONG KONG TOURISM BOARD

'Copy' Items

As you walk down Nathan Road along the spine of the Kowloon peninsula, you are almost certain to be asked if you would like a 'copy watch' or 'copy handbag'. You should be wary of this. It is illegal to sell such items openly and you will be shown photographs of them – always high-end brands.

If you are interested, you will be asked to accompany the salesman to a back street or apartment somewhere. For obvious reasons you should be alert to this. You may not necessarily be robbed, but certainly if you buy such a copy you will have no comeback. If it is not quite what you expected, you will have little chance of finding the seller again.

Getting Information

Hong Kong has a very well respected police force with a good reputation. Most policemen and women speak reasonably good English and are very willing to help with directions and information.

There are Tourist Information counters at the Arrivals building at Hong Kong International Airport, where you can pick up brochures and leaflets.

A very well-resourced Visitor Information Center on the Tsim Sha Tsui concourse of the Star Ferry terminal is open daily from 08:00 until 21:00 (Telephone 2508 1234). You can book tours and hotels from here as well as picking up maps, leaflets and free advice.

English Media

If you want to keep up with the news, there are two daily English language newspapers - the Hong Kong Standard and the South China Morning Post (SCMP). The Standard is now a free paper handed to commuters at strategic points on their journeys. It has some news coverage and lots of advertisements.

The SCMP is considered to be a serious and trusted paid-for newspaper with a high standard of reporting of local, international and Chinese affairs.

The newspapers in Hong Kong, both in Chinese and English have a reputation for fair and unbiased reporting and indeed freedom of the press is protected under article 27 of the Hong Kong Basic Law.

Some commentators however think that criticism of the Mainland in the press has been toned down.

There are two English language television channels run by rival companies. TVB Pearl broadcasts news, children's programs, movies and lifestyle shows. ATV World also broadcasts news, as well as US and UK sit coms and documentaries. Some programs are in Cantonese.

RTHK radios 3 and 4 are in English and broadcast 24 hours a day. The first is a news/current affairs channel and the second plays mainly classical music.

Currency

Hong Kong is one of the largest financial centers in the world and headquarters of famous global banks such as the Hong Kong and Shanghai Banking Corporation (HSBC) and the Standard Chartered Bank. It is not surprising that it has a strong currency.

The Hong Kong dollar is pegged to the US dollar and as such it is relatively stable and fluctuations tend to be minor. It is the thirteenth most traded currency in the world.

Bank notes are issued by HSBC, the Standard Chartered Bank and the Bank of China.

They come in dollar denominations of 10 (purple), 20 (blue), 50 (green), 100 (red), 500 (brown) and 1000 (orange). Due to forgery issues, 1000 notes are now relatively rare and some smaller outlets prefer not to take them.

Silver coins come in 10, 5, 2 and 1 dollar values and there are small denomination brass coins for 50, 20 and 10 cents.

Climate

Hong Kong has a sub-tropical climate with seasonal variations. It has cool winters and hot, humid summers. Winter temperatures can fall to as low as 8 °C Celsius (46 °F).

It is warm, sunny and dry in the autumn and hot, humid and rainy from spring to summer.

The summer months from May until September can get uncomfortably hot with temperatures up to 34 °C (93 °F) and high percentages of humidity. The wettest month is May and the driest is January. The average annual rainfall is 2638.3 mm (103.9 inches).

Hong Kong is a busy tourist destination throughout the year but the most pleasant weather is often in the months of October and November. This is when the humidity drops and the days often become warm and sunny. The least comfortable months are July and August.

Hong Kong suffers from severe rainstorms as well as occasional typhoons. The government has installed sophisticated warning systems for heavy rain and typhoons. Numbered warning signals are issued by the Hong Kong Observatory and hoisted in government buildings, together with appropriate recommendations depending on the proximity of the center or eye of the typhoon. The word 'typhoon' is from the Cantonese *tai fung* – meaning big wind.

Local newspapers, television and radio stations also keep people informed of its progress if a typhoon is in the area, and the Observatory publishes frequent weather updates. (www.hko.gov.hk)

Educational institutions close when an '8' signal is raised and people are advised to stay at home or at their workplace until it is lowered.

Demographics

The population of the territory stands at approximately 7.3 million, according to figures issued by the Census and Statistics Department in 2015.

The population is predominantly ethnic Chinese (92%) with significant minorities from all over the world. The largest of the minority groups comprise 2 % each for Filipinos and Indonesians, 1% South Asians (Indian, Pakistani and Nepalese) 0.4% British and slightly smaller numbers of North Americans, Australians, Thai and Japanese.

There are small communities from numerous other places in the world and Hong Kong remains something of a melting pot where you can come across people from all corners of the Earth.

Many large international corporations have their Far East operations headquartered here, and professionals are attracted by lucrative packages. Before the handover the British population was larger with many long term expatriates, as well as backpackers taking advantage of easily renewed year-long working visas.

Women from the Philippines and more recently Indonesia and Sri Lanka provide vital domestic service and child care to the working middle class. They are mainly employed as live-in domestic helpers on two-year renewable contracts and their regular remittances are welcome additions to the less than buoyant economies of their home countries.

If you are in the Statue Square area in Central near the HSBC headquarters on any Sunday you will hear the boisterous chatter of the hard working girls who congregate there to enjoy their one day off in the week. You will hear them long before you see them!

There is a significant South Asian population, especially living in the Nathan Road area of Kowloon. Many Indians are employed in the tailoring or precious stone industries. You might also come across some fluent Cantonese speaking Sikhs, working in elite hotels. Some of these can trace their ancestry back to the early colonial days when Punjabi Sikhs were recruited by the British Army and the newly formed Hong Kong Police Force.

Hong Kong has a thriving middle class as well as a very wealthy elite. An often quoted statistic is that Hong Kong has more Rolls Royce cars per head of population than anywhere else in the world, and certainly the territory has more than its share of tycoons.

The cost of living is high however, and there is another side to Hong Kong. An estimated 20% of the population struggle to make ends meet, living near or below the official poverty line for a single person of HK$3275 (US$422) per month.

Hong Kong has the highest income gap between rich and poor of any developed economy in the world, and one in three seniors struggle financially.

The Cantonese Dialect

The locally spoken Chinese dialect is Cantonese. This is also spoken in the major Southern Chinese city of Guangzhou (formerly Canton) just 70 miles to the north, and in other parts of neighboring Guangdong province.

The national language of China is Mandarin which is quite different.

Chinese people from different linguistic areas may not understand each other's speech but the written form of the language (either using traditional or simplified characters) is universally understood.

There has been a recent influx of Mainland Chinese settling in Hong Kong and tourism from the Mainland has boomed since the dramatic expansion of the Chinese economy, so you are very likely to hear Mandarin spoken.

It is also the preferred second language in the numerous international English medium schools and it is the language spoken by the greatest number of people in the world.

Public announcements are made in Cantonese, English and Mandarin and many local people can converse in all three.

Cantonese is not an easy language to learn for the Westerner. Although most Cantonese words are single syllable, the dialect uses eight distinct tones, which are often quite hard to distinguish to the untrained ear. Many expatriates learn some survival phrases and a few are listed here, using 'pin yin' phonetics.

jo-sahn – good morning

neh ho mah ? – how are you?

gai do cheen ah? – how much is it?

d'jun jaw – turn left

d'jun yau – turn right

yee doh – stop here

m'goy – thank you

There are many Cantonese phrase books available if you have a good ear for languages and would like to learn more. Locals will be impressed.

Conveniently, a significant number of Hongkongers can speak English to some degree - although in parts of the New Territories this is not always the case. In hotels, shops and restaurants English is widely spoken and understood.

The British influence is still very much in evidence in street signs and place names and it is quite rare to find written signs or public information that is not in Chinese characters accompanied by an English translation.

Street Names

Hong Kong's street names are interesting. Historically they were often given the English name first and then approximations in Cantonese, for example Perth Street became *Ba-fu Guy* and Coxes Road *Cok-tse Doh*.

Past governors, politicians and British royals are well remembered. Lockhart, Nathan and Hennessy were all Hong Kong Governors and streets named for them are major thoroughfares in Wan Chai, Tsim Sha Tsui, and Causeway Bay respectively.

British royals are well represented. If you drive from the Prince of Wales Hospital in Sha Tin, you might journey along Princess Margaret Road, passing within a short distance of Prince Edward MTR station on your way to the Queen Elizabeth Stadium, (by-passing Queen Victoria Park).

Many of the old colonials were clearly nostalgic for home. In the Kowloon Tong district, Cornwall Street is close to Somerset Road and Dorset Road (all English counties). The Scottish are well represented in Kowloon City - on the way to Perth Street you might pass along Forfar Road, Stirling Avenue or Dunbar Street. All of these names have Cantonese approximations with similar sounds but totally random meanings.

Air Pollution

Hong Kong's air pollution is an increasing cause for concern.

The government has taken some steps to reduce it, including the introduction of liquid petroleum gas for taxis and incentives for owners of electric and hybrid cars.

There are still many polluting diesel vehicles and coal is burned at major power stations.

This, together with dirty air blowing over in certain weather conditions from China, can cause serious problems for anyone with respiratory issues.

The government closely monitors the air quality at specific road side stations and the pollution index and forecast is broadcast on radio, television and in the newspapers.

You can also check the government air quality health index on its website www.aqhi.gov.hk

If you do become ill during your stay, your hotel will be able to recommend an English speaking doctor, whose services should be covered by your travel insurance.

In extreme circumstances you will be seen at the nearest Accident and Emergency hospital department. In emergencies call 999.

Health Issues

Since the 2003 outbreak of Severe Acute Respiratory Syndrome (SARS) and some isolated cases of avian flu soon afterwards, there have been no major health issues in the territory.

All arriving passengers, whether by train, boat or plane pass by a thermal scan which automatically takes their temperatures.

Passengers with pneumonia or high fever may have to undergo a more extensive health check and will be closely monitored or even detained.

People travelling from countries which have current epidemics must undergo stringent checks.

Hongkongers have become very health conscious since the SARS outbreak and it is common to see hand sanitizers in toilets, hotels and other public places. Locals with coughs or colds will often wear surgical face masks in public.

Spitting in public has been officially banned - also a direct result of the SARS outbreak. It carries the same fine as littering, which is HK$1500 (US$193) and it is now rarely seen.

Public Toilets

Most MTR and bus stations do not have public toilets but you are unlikely to be far from one in the urban areas. They can be found in most shopping malls, coffee shops and restaurants. An army of unsung heroes keep the many municipal roadside facilities clean. In some areas you might still find traditional 'squat' toilets but most are what you are used to, with adequate hand washing and drying facilities.

Food Safety and Water

Hong Kong's food has an excellent reputation and is usually cooked with fresh ingredients.

Even the roadside *dai pai dongs* have a high standard of hygiene and you should have no gastric problems. If your stomach is more sensitive than most, you might want to avoid oysters and other shellfish.

Some cuts of meat that might be discarded elsewhere are readily available here, as nothing is wasted.

If you like to try new foods, there are plenty of opportunities!

Some of the cheaper restaurants use MSG in their ingredients and you should ask if you are sensitive to this. Peanut oil may also be used and those with peanut allergies should check before ordering.

Unless the plumbing in your building is very old, it is safe to drink tap water. Your hotel will probably provide you with bottled water, however, and it can be cheaply bought at all convenience stores and supermarkets.

Time and Daylight Hours

Hong Kong's position is 22.4° North and 114.11° East. It has a relatively small change in the number of daylight hours from 11 in midwinter to 13.5 in midsummer- there are no long, light evenings here.

It is in the Coordinated Universal Time zone +8, which means it is eight hours ahead of London in winter and 7 in summer. There is no daylight saving scheme in operation.

Consulates

Over 100 countries have official representatives in Hong Kong. There are 61 Consulates-General and 59 Consulates. If you mislay your passport or need to get advice/urgent information relevant to your home country, use the government website to find its contact details. Please visit: www.protocol.gov.hk/ eng/consular/index

Electrical Outlets

Hong Kong uses 220-240 volt electricity and three pin square ended plugs, similar to Britain.

Adapters are available from hotel housekeeping departments or convenience stores.

All but the most basic hotels will have tea and coffee making facilities and Wi-Fi access. Most bathrooms are equipped with a 110 volt and 220 volt two-point socket suitable for electric shavers. Do not worry if you have forgotten anything, it is very likely to be easily attained locally.

Tipping

Tipping is generally expected, although not compulsory, in restaurants, hotels and on taxis.

Anything less than HK$20 would be insulting to a hotel porter who has carried your bag up to your room, but HK$10 is acceptable to the doorman who holds the taxi door open for you. You should also leave something for the maid who has serviced your room and for a stay of 5 or 6 nights, HK$100 is appropriate if you have been well looked after.

Many (but not all) restaurants automatically add a 10% service charge to your bill, but it is by no means certain that the money goes to the waiting staff. If you have been well served you should consider a 5-10 percent addition to this.

On short taxi rides it is appropriate to round up the fare to the nearest dollar. Give a 5 dollar tip for a longer ride.

Credit Cards and Money Exchange

All major credit cards (Visa, American Express, and MasterCard) are accepted in hotels, shopping malls, and in most of the shops in busy shopping districts such as Tsim Sha Tsui, Causeway Bay, Central and Sha Tin.

You can also use these cards to pay for your meals in the larger restaurants and bars.

In small, family run shops and eating establishments, cash is still preferred.

There are numerous ATM machines in main streets and in the concourse of most MTR stations.

Banks are open from 09:30 until 16:30 from Monday to Friday and until 13:00 on Saturdays. Most banks have currency exchange services but you can also find small independent money changing kiosks in the tourist areas, often staying open until late. The rates are clearly shown for comparison purposes. Prices quoted in this book are in Hong Kong dollars (HK$).

Rates of course will fluctuate but at the time of writing there were approximately HK$7.75 to US$1 and HK$11 to one UK pound.

Festivals and Celebrations

Hong Kong has a wealth of colorful festivals and - if your visit coincides with one of the following - you might well want to experience it.

Apart from Christmas, the dates of these festivals vary each year depending on where they fall in the Chinese lunar calendar. Check the Hong Kong tourism website for exact information.

Christmas
Although adopted from the time of British rule, Christmas is still widely celebrated and shops and offices are gaily decorated both inside and out. The

impressive Christmas lights on the sides of tall buildings can been seen from either side of the harbor.

The inevitable piped music appears in major stores and supermarkets as early as November and large shopping malls have lavish central displays, often with Santa Claus grottoes.

The somewhat over-the-top moving diorama outside Ocean Terminal shopping mall, near the Tsim Sha Tsui terminus of Star Ferry is eagerly anticipated and very well photographed.

Chinese New Year.

The most anticipated date in the Hong Kong calendar is the Lunar New Year. This occurs at the first moon of the lunar calendar – usually in late January or early February. The Chinese zodiac is divided into twelve years each named after an animal.

All Hong Kong children know the story of the Jade Emperor's suggestion of a race between the animals across the river to decide how the twelve years should be named. The rat climbed on the ox's nose and jumped ashore first. His is the first year, followed by ox, tiger, rabbit, dragon, snake, horse, goat, monkey, rooster, dog and boar. The sequence then begins again.

According to Chinese astrology, the animal year in which you were born gives you certain characteristics, which may or may not be compatible with other animals.

Some people take this very seriously and may even plan the birth of their children for specific 'auspicious'

years. The year 2000, for example saw an increase in the Hong Kong birth rate as the new millennium coincided with the lucky 'Year of the Dragon.'

There are specific rituals associated with Chinese New Year, including sweeping the house and buying new shoes, but essentially it is a time for visiting family. The airport and the train to China become really busy especially at the beginning of the three day holiday.

The lucky colors of the Lunar New Year are red and gold, and homes and work places are brightly decorated.

Children, unmarried women and people working as security guards, cleaners, and so on, are given small red envelopes containing new crisp bank notes. These are the famous lucky *lai see* packets.

The greeting passed from person to person is *"kung hei fat choi"* – "I wish you good fortune".

There are always Chinese New Year parades and a very impressive firework display where the fireworks are set off from barges in the harbor and their sequence is synchronized to rousing music.

You will also see colorful dragon dances and lion dances. Troupes of dancers go from shop to shop to perform, give good fortune and receive lucky money.

You will probably hear them before they come into view, as the dance is accompanied by loud drumming and the clashing of cymbals.

Mid-Autumn festival

Sometimes called 'lantern festival', this is an ancient celebration of the harvest and has been celebrated by Chinese folk for more than 2000 years. The date coincides with the full moon between early September and early October.

It is a colorful family occasion where groups meet together in public places to share food, light candles and parade with their lanterns (these days they're likely to be battery powered with all sorts of colors and gadgets!)

Victoria Park, Kowloon Park and Sha Tin waterfront are all good places to experience the festival, but it occurs in parks and open spaces all over the territory.

The favored delicacies associated with the festival are 'mooncakes' which come in all shapes and sizes. They are made with pastry surrounding a red bean or lotus seed paste cooked around a hard boiled duck's egg yolk (symbolizing the moon). People are rarely indifferent about the taste of mooncakes and either love or hate them.

Dragon Boat Races

These are also colorful annual events associated with the moon, which take place on the fifth day of the fifth lunar month (usually in late May or early June). The Chinese name is Teung Ng and the festival goes back as far as the third century.

Twenty paddlers sit in pairs and energetically propel the long, narrow wooden boat with short single bladed paddles. A drummer or caller faces the paddlers and a steersman stands at the back of the boat and uses a longer paddle as a tiller. Races are fiercely competitive. Training starts long before the big day and some of the biggest races are held at Sha Tin, Stanley and Sai Kung. Flags and strings of bunting are prepared to add to the atmosphere. Later in the year, Hong Kong hosts International races. The sport is very popular and recently has been developed to include female and mixed crews. It also attracts expatriate participants.

Cheung Chau Bun Festival

This is a lesser known, but equally colorful, festival which is unique to the small Outlying Island of Cheung Chau. Legend has it that the festival originated after the island was decimated by a plague which killed thousands. The plague was only defeated when some islanders fetched the god Pak Tai to drive the evil spirits away.

Pak Tai is remembered every year with an ornate parade including lion dances, floats and martial arts demonstrations. The festival culminates with the climbing of a bamboo 'mountain' set up beforehand. This is erected near the temple and is covered with hand-made buns. The Cheung Chau activities take place during the week after the Buddha's birthday, usually early to mid- May.

Getting There

Getting to Hong Kong is easy - it is extremely well connected by its international airport to most of the world and can be accessed by other means too.

Flights

The majority of visitors arrive by plane at Hong Kong International Airport (Chek Lap Kok) on Lantau Island. More than 68 million passengers and 4.38 million tonnes of cargo passed through the airport in 2015 and it is not an exaggeration to say that it runs like clockwork.

There are direct flights to Hong Kong from major cities in Asia, Europe, Africa, North America and Oceania and by transfer from almost everywhere else. All of the world's major airlines have connections with Hong Kong.

The local Hong Kong owned flagship carrier is Cathay Pacific and it operates more than 140 planes flying worldwide. Its subsidiary, Dragonair specializes in flights to China and has more than 40 passenger aircraft.

Several budget airlines are also headquartered here, including Hong Kong Airlines, Hong Kong Express and Air Hong Kong.

Hong Kong International Airport handles 68 flights per hour at peak times and 1,100 daily. There are nearly 300 retail shops and 60 catering outlets in the two terminals.

More than half of the World's population live within a five hour flight from Hong Kong, and over 73,000 people work at the airport.

The shortest approximate flight times in hours from some major cities are: New York 16.5, Toronto 16, Cape Town 15.5, London 12.5, Auckland 12, Cairo 10.5, Moscow 9.5, Sydney 9 and Dubai 8.

Transfer from the Airport

The transport links to and from the airport also run efficiently. Follow the clear signs at one of the two arrival halls for the Airport Express. This railway is operated the Hong Kong Mass Transit Railway (MTR) and was built on reclaimed land running along the shore of North Lantau. High speed trains shuttle to Kowloon and Central where you will arrive in just 24 minutes.

Airport double decker buses are operated by New World First Bus Company (a subsidiary of Citibus) and connect to centers all over the territory. This is the least expensive option.

If you are catching a taxi, follow the sign and a helpful airport employee stationed there will ask for your destination and direct you to the correct queue.

Many of the upper end hotels will arrange an airport transfer directly to your hotel and you will be met after you have passed through Customs. If you wish, a limousine and driver can be hired upon arrival.

Whichever way you leave the airport it is likely to be quick and efficient.

Other Routes

Other visitors to Hong Kong might arrive by boat – perhaps by one of the hover ferries from Macau or one of the other Chinese ports.

Many cruise ships include Hong Kong on their Far East itinerary and these berth at Ocean Terminal on the Tsim Sha Tsui waterfront, close to Star Ferry.

Many Mainland visitors will arrive at Kowloon's Hung Hom station from the direct rail link with Guangzhou . There are also several cross border bus routes.

Hiring a Car

Although you will probably have a smooth drive along the Lantau freeway after leaving the airport complex, don't be deceived.

Hong Kong's urban roads can get very congested and the number of privately owned vehicles in the territory recently passed the half million mark.

This represents 63 cars for every 1000 people living in the territory, which is relatively few when compared with other cities – Singapore has 100 and London 300. Owning a car is expensive in Hong Kong, not just the purchase, registration tax and annual road license but also crippling parking fees. In a compact area where millions of journeys are made each day, owning a car is a financial burden, as well as a source of pollution.

It is possible to hire a car in Hong Kong but parking restrictions and excess insurance requirements make this a very costly undertaking.

If there is a good public transport system it makes sense to do without a private car, and Hong Kong's public transport is among the best in the world. There are few places which are inaccessible by bus, train, tram, ferry or taxi and transport costs are very reasonable.

Transportation

Hopefully the previous chapter has convinced you that hiring a car is not a necessity in Hong Kong - and in fact is not recommended. Instead, you should explore Hong Kong using its world class public transportation system.

Public Transport: Octopus Card

If you are staying in Hong Kong for more than a few days it is worth obtaining an 'octopus' card. These are available at Customer Service desks at MTR stations for a refundable HK$50 deposit. They can be loaded with cash at machines in the station or at the numerous convenience stores (7 Eleven, Circle K). You can use them on trains, ferries, buses and green minibuses and also buy drinks and snacks at the convenience stores with them.

Taxis

Taxis are plentiful and convenient in Hong Kong and by the standards of other developed countries quite inexpensive, especially for short rides.

They come in three colors depending upon where you travel. The light blue taxis are fairly sparse as they only serve Lantau Island. The green taxis operate in the New Territories, and the largest number are the urban red taxis. Only certain taxis may access certain areas. If your first experience of hiring a cab is at the airport, just tell the taxi steward your destination and he/she will guide you.

All taxis have meters which are strictly used. Your fare will be clearly displayed throughout the journey. Fares for urban cabs start at HK$22 for the first 2km and HK$1.60 for each 200m after that. The fares for New Territories' cabs are HK$18.50 and HK$1.40 for the same distances, and Lantau taxis are slightly cheaper. Remember you have to pay the toll for tunnel crossings and bags stored in the trunk are charged HK$5 each - these are extra and will not be included in the price displayed on the meter.

Most taxi drivers are honest, but very rarely a driver might try to take advantage of your ignorance of the streets by taking you on a roundabout route to gain a higher fare. Names and license numbers are clearly displayed, with a telephone number and complaints procedure. By law you must wear your seat belt.

Hong Kong cab drivers may not understand English too well and to avoid confusion, ask one of the reception staff at your hotel to write your destination in Chinese. Don't forget to always carry your hotel name card to make your return journey simple.

Double Decker Buses

Unlike the government resourced MTR, several bus companies in Hong Kong are privately owned and provide franchised services across the territory, operating more than 700 routes with nearly 6,000 buses.

The largest of these is the Kowloon Motor Bus Company (1933) which is so proud of its history that it incorporates its founding year in its name! KMB operates 3,800 air conditioned buses mainly in Kowloon and the New Territories.

Citibus operates another 1,000 buses on 100 routes on Hong Kong Island and the Airport Buses through its subsidiary New World First Bus.

On all buses, you pay on entry either by cash (no change is given) or by using an octopus card.

Although passengers may stand downstairs if all seats are full, you cannot stand upstairs. Buses invariably leave their origin on time but traffic jams are not uncommon, with associated delays.

There are, in fact, certain notorious bottle necks such as the Cross-Harbor or Eastern Harbor tunnels and traffic can be seriously delayed there, especially if there is an accident or breakdown. Unlike the rest of China, the traffic in Hong Kong drives on the left as in Britain.

Many busy routes have lanes designated for buses only - some lanes operating only during rush hours. There are some cross-harbor bus routes which are convenient but slightly more expensive.

An X after the bus number denotes an express service with limited stops. The 6X from Central bus station to Stanley on the south side of Hong Kong Island, for example will take about 30 minutes and cost HK$8.50.

Double decker buses have a flat fare, regardless of the distance of your journey. Most drivers speak at least some English.

Public Light Minibuses are plentiful and come in two colors, green and red. They shuttle between their specific routes for a set fare. You pay as you board, either by depositing your cash into a box or by touching your octopus

card. They contain just 16 seats and standing is strictly forbidden.

Often the driver will wait for the bus to be almost full before setting off, on what can sometimes be a 'white-knuckle' ride. Once moving the drivers do not delay!

These minibuses are quicker than double-deckers and a little (but not much) more expensive. On all but the very latest models, which have bells installed, you will have to shout to the driver to stop for you. Give him plenty of warning. He will understand, "'next bus stop please," but it's a good opportunity to practice your Cantonese *"Ba Tse Djam, M'goy"*.

Don't be too quiet, if he/she hears you a hand will be raised in acknowledgement.

The Mass Transit Railway (MTR)

The MTR underground rail system was opened in 1979 with the short stretch between Shep Kip Mei and Kwun Tong on Kowloon side. The first train ran beneath the harbor the following year to connect with newly opened Central station and others along the Island Line.

Since the early days, extensions have been added to the system and new lines opened and there are now 87 MTR stations including those on the Airport Express. There are an additional 68 stops on the Light Rail Transit (LRT) in the northern New Territories.

The most recent stations are Ho Man Tin and Whampoa which extended the Kwun Tong line on Kowloon side and began operation in October 2016.

The MTR is the envy of many other subway systems around the world and consistently achieves a staggering 99.9% on-time rate on its train journeys. When you travel on the MTR you will be surprised to learn that parts of it are nearly forty years old - it appears much newer.

There is no graffiti in the carriages and no rubbish on the floor. It is spotlessly clean despite being used daily by millions. Signs and announcements tell you that eating or drinking beyond the ticket barriers are forbidden and the overwhelming majority of commuters do as they are asked. Consequently there are no discarded food wrappers.

The MTR connects many areas of the territory quickly and directly and it is very likely that you will use it during your stay.

There are easily understood interconnected color coded lines and information maps are displayed on the trains and at the stations both in English and Chinese. Announcements and information is clearly given in Cantonese, Mandarin and English and station attendants are very willing to help you with directions.

Lights on the map displays in the carriages mark your progress and even indicate the side where the sliding doors will open as the train reaches a station. The trains run from 06:00 until approximately 01:00 the next morning.

Fares are kept comparatively low. For example a 27 minute ride from Hang Hau in the East of the New Territories to Admiralty near Central, traveling beneath the harbor, changing lines at North Point and passing 10 stops, will cost you HK$14 (US$1.80). Fares vary with the length of the journey.

If you don't have an Octopus card, you can buy a single ticket at the machines in the station concourse. The machines have an English as well as a Chinese option. There are also special tourist day passes available at the Customer Services desks (HK$65). Check the web site for up to date information. www.mtr.com.hk/ en/customer/tickets/ travel_pass

The MTR does, of course, get very crowded and you should try to avoid rush hours if you don't want an uncomfortable journey. These are between 07:00 and 10:30 in the mornings and 16:00 and 19:30 in the evening. Certain key stations, however, can get extremely busy at any time – for example Admiralty, Kowloon Tong, Mong Kok and Tsim Sha Tsui. If you travel during rush hours, be prepared to be inadvertently jostled.

Extra staff are employed at these stations during busy periods to ensure safe alighting and departing. Hongkongers do have a culture of queueing in a reasonable and civilized fashion and most commuters will wait on either side of the sliding door area to let passengers off, before they board.

Buses and minibuses often connect with MTR stations – a letter M after the bus number means it goes to at least one MTR station. If you do get lost when walking the Hong Kong streets, you can often regain your bearings by finding the nearest MTR station. The logo is

very familiar and widely displayed above ground.

Before it amalgamated with the MTR, there was another railway company in Hong Kong which had a much longer history. This was the Kowloon Canton Railway (KCR) which ran a regular service from Hung Hom station in Kowloon via the New Territories satellite towns of Sha Tin, Tai Po and Fanling to the border post of Lo Wu, where foot passengers then traverse the bridge to Chinese Customs. This line is now called MTR East Rail and apart from the tunnel between Kowloon Tong and Tai Wai, it travels above ground.

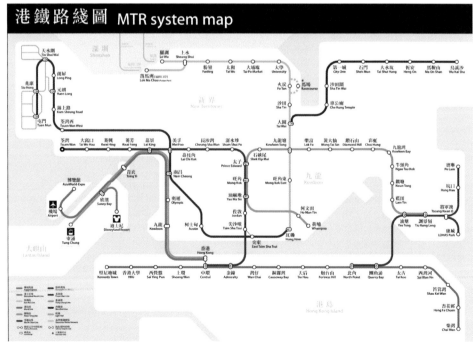

港鐵路綫圖 MTR system map

Cross Border Trains

As previously mentioned, the MTR East Rail trains run up to the Chinese border and at Lo Wu or Lok Ma Chau stations travelers can, if they have an appropriate visa, enter the Chinese city of Shenzhen. An alternative is to catch the cross border train straight through to Guangzhou.

The train starts at Hung Hom Station in Kowloon and takes about ninety minutes. All formalities are completed before your journey. If you have time, a few days in China will give you a different perspective.

Hong Kong Tramways

Where else in the world can you jump on a slow moving double decker tram and view the daily goings on of some of the busiest streets in the world? However brief your visit to Hong Kong, you must have at least one electric tram ride.

The first electric tram trundled along the tracks in 1910 and they have been carrying passengers along their routes near the north shore of Hong Kong Island ever since.

The trams have been modernized but give a similar experience as in times long gone. They are cheap, colorful and the most environmentally friendly form of mass transport in town. The lines run between Shau Kei Wan in the east to Kennedy Town in the west with a branch that circles Happy Valley.

You can hop on and off at stops which are about 250 meters apart and the linear journey takes about 90 minutes. Both termini have MTR stations nearby and pass others en-route. (There is no MTR station at Happy Valley). It is the only tram system in the world which uses double decker carriages and is well loved by locals and tourists alike.

The trams get their 'ding-ding' nickname from locals for the distinctive bell the driver uses to warn jaywalkers of its quiet approach. You get on at the back and pay as you exit at the front either by cash (HK$2.30) or by touching your octopus card.

Trams do get very busy during rush hours but at other times they should be a 'must-do' on your Hong Kong itinerary.

Sitting upstairs at the front gives visitors a unique view of some of the most densely populated parts of the Island at the leisurely pace of about 11km/h.

As well as just experiencing the trip, or getting easily, if slowly, from one place to another as locals do, it is also possible to book a tour on a genuine 1920s open top tram. This offers a link between Hong Kong's fascinating history and its modern culture. Other private functions can be arranged through the company such as a 'tram party'.

There are two other examples of Hong Kong transport which are covered in the next chapter as they are tourist attractions in their own right. These are the 'Star' Ferry and The Peak Tram.

Neighbourhood Guides

Hong Kong is very much a tourist friendly destination and most, if not all, of the attractions mentioned in this book are well signposted. In many cases they are near MTR stations and your most straightforward route will be by MTR. Before leaving the station concourse look for the attraction listed on the exit boards for the closest lettered exit. You will often find blue or pink direction signs above the ground. If you do get lost, just ask a local. Of course a street map will be helpful and you can pick up a free map at the airport or Tourist Information Office.

As we look through each neighborhood, we have included a brief description and history of the area, a look at accommodation options, along with popular attractions and places to eat. Organizing the guide in this manner allows you to find a neighborhood you like, and then find local places to stay and dine.

Each attraction, restaurant and accommodation listed features a fact sheet with symbols, the key below helps to explain what each of these symbols means.

 Nearest MTR station

 Opening Hours

 Address

 Website

 Entry price in HK$

 Phone number

Hong Kong by Neighborhood

Hong Kong is full of surprises around every corner and each neighbourhood offers something unique to explore.

This chapter offers a brief description of the main tourist neighborhoods, including some suggestions of places to eat and drink, and stay. Of course tastes will vary and although recommendations are offered in good faith, you will of course make your own judgements and your experience may be entirely different to ours. Of the seven neighborhoods discussed, three are in Kowloon, three are on Hong Kong Island and one (Sha Tin) is in the New Territories.

Before detailing the areas, here are some generic comments.

Hotels

Hong Kong has more than 250 licensed hotels and you will be guided by your own preferences as to area and cost. At the end of each of the neighborhood sections we include examples of hotels in or near the neighborhood, in luxury, mid-range and budget categories.

The prices quoted in Hong Kong dollars, are for a twin sharing room and may or may not include breakfast. They are approximations at one point in time and may have changed when you read this. We suggest that you shop around the various hotel search engines for the best value. You will want to make the most of your visit to Hong Kong and it is important to find a hotel that is reasonably convenient for some of the places you would like to see.

Having said that, the Hong Kong transport system is such that most areas are reasonably accessible if not by MTR then by bus and certainly taxi. Perhaps your most important decision is whether you want to be on the Hong Kong or Kowloon side.

There are hotels and guest houses to suit all budgets, often within walking distance of each other. The historic and luxurious Peninsula Hotel (HK$3500 per night) is just ten minutes by foot along Nathan Road from the equally well known, but rather more notorious Chungking Mansions, where rooms of dubious cleanliness can be hired for HK$150 a night.

Fast Food

Like many metropolitan areas of the world, there is a large choice of fast food available in Hong Kong. There are familiar Western establishments as well as three local chains.

Western fast food chains such as McDonalds, KFC and Pizza hut and Starbucks are available throughout Hong Kong - collectively these chains have over 500 locations. They are a safe bet if you don't want to try any of the local food , but each of these also offers dishes tailored to Hong Kong's tastes.

There are three local chains where you can try fast food with a Cantonese twist. These are Café de Coral, Fairwood and Maxim's. You will find branches in all the major shopping centers. The food is quick, but includes fresh ingredients and will give you an initial taste of local cuisine. Menus are in English as well as in Chinese.

In some places you order and pay first and collect your food at a different counter - just watch the locals. Many of the dishes are variations on barbecued meat, rice and vegetables and often include soup. Filling meals typically cost less than HK$50, and they tend to be somewhat healthier than their Western counterparts.

Although you can often get good value meals in Hong Kong, especially at lunchtime, alcoholic drinks tend to be expensive. In some hotel coffee shops, for example, your drinks are likely to be almost as expensive as your meal. If you ask for water, you will often be offered expensive mineral water. Tap water is free and quite drinkable, but you need to request it specifically.

Open Rice
This is an extensive food and restaurant guide website, which may be useful in your search for places to eat in Hong Kong. Established over ten years ago, it publishes users' reviews of different restaurants in various neighborhoods. It also gives comprehensive directions to find the restaurant, as well as a price guide and information about the menus. The website is: www.openrice.com/en/hongkong

Chopsticks
To get the most of your visit to Hong Kong, you should try some of the local Cantonese restaurants, where you will be given chopsticks. Plates of food are shared and the chopsticks allow you to pick from different items for your own bowl. Often the table will be circular and the food placed on an inner revolving circular glass platform.

You should be aware if others are reaching for food before rotating this in your direction. It is quite acceptable to hold your bowl up to your mouth and to use the chopsticks to scoop, for example rice, into your mouth. Many restaurants now use longer chopsticks purely for serving.

It is good manners to place choice items into the bowl of guests, or elders. It is impolite to spear food with a chopstick. To use them correctly, you keep the lower chopstick still, resting on the thumb and between fingers.

The upper chopstick is held like a pencil and food is held in a pincer grip as it is moved towards the stationary one. Practice at home with peanuts!

A. Tsim Sha Tsui (TST)

Tsim Sha Tsui is a major tourist area in Hong Kong. It is at the tip of the Kowloon peninsula and it is from here that Star Ferry crosses the harbor to Central. Many museums are within reach, as well as the Avenue of the Stars, Kowloon Park and the Hong Kong Cultural Centre. There is a very pleasant waterfront promenade in TST as well as upmarket shopping malls, such as Harbor City, Ocean Terminal and I Square.

The main spine of TST is Nathan Road which starts near the waterfront opposite the Space Museum and runs for approximately 3.6 kilometers from south to north and finishes at Sham Shui Po. If you get lost in this part of Kowloon, you won't be far from Nathan Road and five MTR stations have entrances in it (Tsim Sha Tsui, Jordan, Yau Ma Tei, Mong Kok and Prince Edward).

TST has some of the most expensive hotels in Hong Kong including The Peninsula, which has amazing views over the harbor. This historic hotel with its Colonial atmosphere and fleet of dark green Rolls Royces was opened in 1928 and it is Hong Kong's oldest hotel.

It is here that the surrender of Hong Kong to the Japanese was signed on Christmas Day in 1941. The hotel had an extension constructed in 1994 which added a 30 floor tower, without changing the recognizable façade.

A favorite for visitors and locals alike is afternoon tea in the Peninsula lobby. This really gives a taste of British Colonial times with dainty sandwiches and pastries served on three tiered trays in elegant surroundings. You can sip the tea of your choice and listen to the Hotel's classical music string quartet.

Attractions

The Hong Kong Museum of Art

 Tsim Sha Tsui, Exit J   Free

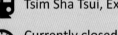 Currently closed for renovation   2721 0116

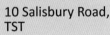 10 Salisbury Road, TST   www.museums.gov.hk/en

The Museum of Art is located along the Tsim Sha Tsui waterfront close to the Cultural Centre and Space Museum. Its displays are mainly paintings and sculptures, with visiting temporary exhibitions of world class standard. It has several renowned galleries of Chinese calligraphy.

At the time of writing it is closed for extensive renovations. Check the web site for its projected re-opening date or call 2721 0116.

Kowloon Park

 Jordan, Exit C

 Free

 05:00 to 24:00

2724 3344

 22 Austin Road, Jordan, TST.

 www.lcsd.gov.hk/en/parks/kp

This pleasant oasis in bustling Kowloon spans one side of Nathan Road between Austin Road and Haiphong Road in TST. It was formerly a British Army barracks and it covers an area of 13.3 hectares.

Kowloon Park includes a tree walk, a rose garden, ornate fountains, a Chinese garden, a bird lake and an aviary. There is also a fitness trail and children's adventure playground. It has one of the busiest outdoor swimming pools in the territory.

Kowloon Park caters to early risers and it is a good place to watch locals performing tai chi and other early morning exercises.

Outside the park near the Nathan Road entrance, you can find some fine examples of Hong Kong's auspicious banyan trees. Nearby is the thought-provoking 'Please' sculpture of one hand clasped upon another.

The 'Star' Ferry

 Tsim Sha Tsui, Exit J or Central, Exit A

 Upper Deck HK$2.50 to HK$3.40. Lower Deck HK$2.00 to HK$2.80.

 Daily from 07:00 to 23:00

 2367 7065

 Star Ferry Pier, Kowloon Point, TST

 www.starferry.com.hk

Everyone who visits Hong Kong should have at least one ride on the historic Star Ferry. If the weather is clear you will get great views of both sides of the harbor. If you travel after dark you will enjoy the neon lights and can get some stunning photographs.

Although there are now road and rail tunnels, in the early days of the British Colony the only method of crossing the harbor was by boat. The Star Ferry Company began its operations in 1888 and its name dates from ten years later.

For well over a century since then it has regularly plied crossings between Tsim Sha Tsui (TST) and Central. Of the two termini, TST is the most historic - the clock tower nearby, which you can enter, dates from 1915. The terminus on Hong Kong side was moved in 2006 - despite considerable protest - to its current location to make way for a reclamation project. Previously it was much closer to the business district near Edinburgh Place and was more convenient for office commuters.

Before 2006 it was still possible to see some of the iconic rickshaws near the Central terminus of Star Ferry, complete with their aging pullers. These elderly men, although not up to operating the ancient conveyances, could still make a useful living exploiting photographic opportunities. Alas the rickshaw 'boys' have now gone, although near the Edinburgh Place car park you might still see one or two of the ancient contraptions, safely padlocked.

Star Ferry is a great trip and costs very little. There is an alternate route which goes from TST to Wan Chai which costs minimally more.

Use your octopus card or cash as you pay on entry. Each of the twelve boats currently in service has 'star' in its name (Morning Star, Meridian Star and so on). The oldest currently operating is Celestial Star which dates from 1956.

You can choose to sit on the upper or lower deck. The boats can carry between 500 and 600 passengers and run every 10 or 12 minutes.

The upper deck will give you better photo opportunities but if you want to see the seamen berth and cast off with precision and skill, try the lower deck.

The Star Ferry Company also organizes guided tours of the harbor.

The Waterfront at Night – Symphony of Lights Show

 Tsim Sha Tsui, Exit J or Central, Exit A   Free

 20:00 each evening   2810 2770

 The Waterfront, TST & The Waterfront, Central   www.tourism.gov.hk/symphony/english

You will have certainly seen amazing photographs of the Hong Kong skyline and on your visit you must experience this 'sound and light' show along one of the waterfront paths either at Tsim Sha Tsui or across the harbor in Central.

We prefer the TST side where you can see the island, the Central skyscrapers and the Peak beyond, but it's a matter of taste. If you have the time you can do both.

Arrive and find your spot by 7.45pm. On the dot of eight the show will begin. It is sponsored by the Hong Kong Tourist Board and various corporations, and makes use of traditional as well as laser lights to highlight some of the buildings.

The show lasts about 15 minutes and is accompanied by music and an introduction in three languages.

The Avenue of the Stars

 Tsim Sha Tsui, Exit J   Free

 24 hours (currently closed for renovation)   2734 8890

 The Waterfront, TST   www.discoverhongkong.com/eng

The Hong Kong film industry is amongst the five largest in the world. Traditionally it specialized in action/martial arts type films and the two iconic stars who come to mind are Jackie Chan and the late Bruce Lee.

In recent years however Hong Kong has made many films in other, perhaps more sensitive genres and it has given the world many renowned stars.

If you are a cinema fan you should head to the Kowloon East waterfront and you will see the Avenue of the Stars, Hong Kong's version of the Hollywood Walk of Fame.

The avenue was created after Lee's death but he is represented with a life sized statue in typical martial arts pose.

As for Jackie Chan and more than 100 other Hong Kong film stars, they are represented by individual flagstones with handprints and signatures. The attraction is free and you should allow about an hour to see it.

NB: At the time of writing this attraction was closed for renovation, please check the HK tourism board for the re-opening date.

Hong Kong Science Museum

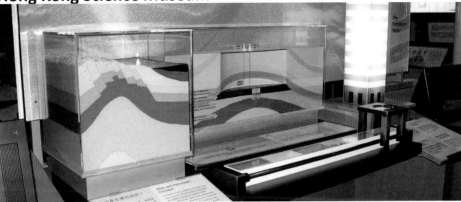

 Tsim Sha Tsui, Exit P

 HK$25 for adults, 1/2 price for children & seniors. Free admission on Wednesdays.

 2732 3232

 10:00 to 19:00 weekdays (Closed Thurs) and 10: 00 to 21:00 at weekends.

 2, Science Museum Road, TST

 www.lcsd.gov.hk/ce/Museum/Science

This is a great place for children and adults alike and it has many displays including an amazing 22 meter high energy machine where large balls are moved around a frame as if by magic.

There are many interactive displays for children including a driving machine, a light and shadow display, computer graphic experiments, optical illusions, life and food science exhibits and a flight simulator.

Aircraft enthusiasts can see Cathay Pacific's first DC3 suspended from the ceiling and there are engines where you can see the moving parts.

It is an excellent museum and well worth a visit, but it gets very busy at weekends. Allow two to three hours.

Museum of History

 Tsim Sha Tsui, Exit P   HK$10

 2724 9042   10:00 to 18:00 weekdays (Closed on Tues) and 10:00 to19:00 at weekends.

 Science Museum Road, TST   www.lcsd.gov.hk/ce/Museum/History

This is next door to the Science Museum and if you have good powers of concentration you could visit them both on the same day (although not on a Tuesday or Thursday) with a break for lunch.

The museum traces the history of the South China area from 400 million years ago to the handover of Hong Kong from Britain to China in 1997.

The Museum has thousands of exhibits, multi-media displays and realistic dioramas (including one of early man in the area).

Adults and children will love boarding the old Chinese Junk replica, viewing the large black and white photographs of agricultural workers from a time long gone and visiting a 1950s Chinese medicine shop.

Allow 2 to 3 hours for your visit.

Hong Kong Space Museum

 Tsim Sha Tsui, Exit J

 Free. Omnimax tickets start at HK$24.

 2721 0226

 Monday to Friday 13:00 to 21:00,
Weekends 10:00 to 21:00. Closed Tues.

 10 Salisbury Road, TST

 www.museums.gov.hk/en

If you are wondering about the unusual windowless domed building on the TST waterfront opposite the end of Nathan Road, it is the Hong Kong Space Museum - another famous architectural landmark in Hong Kong.

Included in this museum is a planetarium, a hall of astronomy, a hall of space science, and a lecture hall and gift shop. Many of the exhibits are interactive.

Part of the museum is an 'Omnimax' theater where space and wildlife films are regularly shown. You sit back in your seat to take in a 180-degree view of the film as it is projected on the hemispheric screen above you. Headphones provide an accompanying commentary in a choice of 4 languages. It is an amazing experience, but wise to book in advance.

Dining

TST has a multitude of bars and restaurants. Many of the hotels have excellent buffet lunches and dinners and some even offer buffet afternoon teas.

In Ashley Road you will find very good bars which also sell food, including Mes Amies and Ned Kelly's Last Stand (which has live jazz).

In Knutsford Terrace, near Kimberley Road there is a pedestrian terrace of bars and restaurants where you can dine al fresco and watch the world go by. Restaurants on The Terrace include Italian, French, Spanish, Japanese, Turkish and Russian. Here are three personal TST favorites.

The Spring Deer
Nearest MTR: *Tsim Sha Tsui*
Address: *42 Mody Road, TST*
Opening Hours: *12:00 to 15:00 and 18:00 to 23:00 daily.*
Phone: *2366 4012*

The Spring Deer is an authentic Pekingese restaurant which is very popular with locals. The signature dish is roast duck which is eaten in doughy pancakes with spring onions and plum sauce. The shredded beef in sesame buns is also very good as are the sizzling prawns. You need to book in advance.

Swagat
Nearest MTR: *Tsim Sha Tsui*
Address: *Shop 103-104 1/F Chungking Mansions, Nathan Road, TST*
Opening Hours: *11:00 to 23:00 daily*
Phone: *2723 7618*

This is a very good, relatively small and inexpensive Indian restaurant on the first floor of Chungking Mansions. There is a wide variety of Indian dishes available, the rogan josh and aloo gobi are especially good. Indian beer is also available.

Delaney's
Nearest MTR: *Tsim Sha Tsui*
Address: *71 Peking Road, TST*
Opening Hours: *08.00 to 02:00 daily.*
Phone: *2301 3980*

Delaney's is an authentic Irish Pub and restaurant which has been in Hong Kong since 1995. As well as Guinness and Irish Beer it serves nourishing Western food including chicken and steak dishes and fish and chips. It is open early for breakfasts and it also shows live televised sport.

Hotels

The Sheraton
Nearest MTR: *Tsim Sha Tsui*
Address: *20 Nathan Road, TST*
Telephone: *2369 1111*
Website: *www. sheratonhongkonghotel. com*

The Sheraton Hotel is in a very convenient location and features an outdoor pool, fitness and massage center, eight dining options and cocktail bar. The 782 rooms are spacious and luxurious and the staff friendly and welcoming. Approximately HK$1800 per night

The Salisbury YMCA
Nearest MTR: *Tsim Sha Tsui*
Address: *41, Salisbury Road, TST.*
Telephone: *2268 7000*
Website: *www.ymcahk. org.hk/thesalisbury/en*

The Salisbury YMCA Hotel is in an excellent location, near to Star Ferry. It has 372 good sized rooms, a fitness center, swimming pool, restaurants and friendly staff - HK$950 per night.

The Guangdong Hotel
Nearest MTR: *Tsim Sha Tsui*
Address: *18, Prat Avenue, TST*
Telephone: *3410 8888*

Website: *www.gdhotel. com.hk*

For a budget hotel you could do worse than the 244 room Guangdong Hotel in Prat Avenue. It is clean and modern and rooms are reasonably priced at about HK$450. It is in a busy shopping area within 5 minutes of TST MTR station.

NB: There are many good quality hotels around the Mody Road area of TST East. This area is well connected by a long underpass to the Nathan Road area and it has an MTR station of its own.

B. Mong Kok/Yau Ma Tei

This area of Kowloon around the north end of Nathan road is rather less affluent than TST, although you can still find some luxurious hotels here. It is in fact one of the most densely populated areas of the world and has an entry for such in the Guinness Book of Records.

It is not the place for you if you want peace and quiet, but if you are fascinated by bustling street life it is worth considering. Here you will be within walking distance of several busy markets, including the night market at Temple Street, the Jade Market, the Flower Market and Bird Street. You will be able to access buses and MTR stations easily and taxis are plentiful.

Dining

In Temple Street you will find some excellent *'dai pai dongs'*, which are humble street side eating establishments. They serve a selection of freshly cooked dishes, including great noodles, which go very well with cold local beer (Tsing Tao is a favorite). Most of the *dai pai dongs* have English versions of their menus, or certainly pictures.

There are several small bars and karaoke establishments along Temple Street. The area is very much a local one and apart from the inevitable fast food outlets you will find few Western restaurants, although there are some in the large shopping malls, notably the 59 floor Langham Place and at Grand Century Plaza near Prince Edward Road.

Tong Tai Restaurant
Nearest MTR: *Jordan*
Address: *184A Temple Street, Jordan*
Opening Hours: *18:00 to 02:30 daily*
Phone: *2384 5269*

This is near the Jordan entrance of Temple Street night market and it sells seafood and traditional Cantonese dishes. You can sit outdoors and watch the people on their way to and from the market. It is well used by locals and the food is fresh and well cooked.

Berliner German Bar and Restaurant
Nearest MTR: *Mong Kok*
Address: *Shop 05, Level 13 Langham Place, 8 Argyle Street, Mong Kok.*
Opening Hours: *12:00 to 01:00 Sunday to Thursday, 12:00 to 02:00 Friday and Saturday*
Phone: *2972 0078*

This is a well-reviewed German restaurant inside the large Langham Place complex. It serves traditional German dishes with good sized portions. The apple strudel is superb.

City Cafe
Nearest MTR: *Yau Ma Tei*
Address: *1/F, The Cityview Hotel, 23, Waterloo Road, Yau Ma Tei*
Opening Hours: *07:00 to 15:00, 18:00 to 23:00 daily.*
Phone: *2783 3287*

This is a hotel restaurant which has won awards for its food. It specializes in buffet meals and is open for breakfast lunch and dinner. There is a wide range of Western and Chinese dishes and it will satisfy the largest of appetites.

Hotels

The Royal Plaza
Nearest MTR: *Mong Kok East*
Address: *193, Prince Edward Road West*
Telephone: *2928 8822*
Website: *www.royalplaza.com.hk*

The Royal Plaza is a luxurious hotel with 699 large and comfortable rooms. It is above a shopping mall with easy access to Mong Kok East MTR station. There is a pool, sauna and massage facilities as well as a fitness center, and several dining choices. Rooms here are about HK$1500.

The Metropark Hotel
Nearest MTR: *Mong Kok*
Address: *75, Waterloo Road, Kowloon*
Telephone: *2761 1711*

The Metropark is a comfortable and spacious hotel with 430 rooms. It has both a Western and Chinese restaurant. Although it is a 15 minute walk to either Yau Ma Tei or Mong Kok MTR stations, if you cross the road you can catch a number 7 bus which travels along Waterloo Road and turns into Nathan Road and terminates at Star Ferry.

At night this is a great trip along the neon lit 'Golden Mile'. Sit upstairs at the front if you can. Rooms here are about HK$660.

Kong Hing Guest House
Nearest MTR: *Mong Kok*
Address: *14/F Sun Hing Building, 607 Nathan Road, Mong Kok*
Telephone: *2362 8859*
Website: *www.booking.com/hotel/hk/new-kong-hing-guest-house.en*

The Kong Hing a comparatively small budget option. It is conveniently located at the Mong Kok end of Nathan Road. It receives positive ratings for cleanliness, staff performance and comfort and is good value at HK$400.

C. Kowloon City

The Kowloon City neighborhood is quite extensive and it includes Hung Hom, Ho Man Tin, Kowloon Tong and Kowloon City. It is to the east and north of Kowloon and includes such attractions as Wong Tai Sin Temple, Nan Lian Garden, Kowloon Walled City Garden and the Whampoa shopping complex.

Attractions

Sky 100 Observation Deck

 Kowloon, Exit C

 2613 3888

 1 Austin Road West, Kowloon.

 Adults: HK$168, Concessions: HK$118. 15% discount if booked online.

 Sun to Thurs 10:00 to 21:00. Fri & Sat 10:00 to 22:00. Last entry 1 hour before closing.

 www.sky100.com.hk

Sky 100 is a relatively new attraction. It is a 360 degree observation platform, situated on the 100th floor of the International Commerce Centre in West Kowloon.

High speed elevators take you up in 60 seconds and on a clear day you will see stunning panoramic views of Hong Kong Island, the Kowloon Peninsula and distant Tai Mo Shan (Hong Kong's highest point).

There are pre-recorded views taken on bright days and interactive touch screen information.

Tickets are not cheap but there is a system for a free re-visit should the weather be so bad that your views are obscured.

Nan Lian Garden and Chi Lin Nunnery

 Diamond Hill

 $ Free

3658 93669 (G)
2354 1888 (N)

  07:00 – 21:00 (G) 09:00 – 16:30 (N)

 See description.

 www.hongkongextras.com

Address: 60 Fung Tak Road, Diamond Hill (Gardens). 5 Chi Lin Road, Diamond Hill (Nunnery)

Close to Diamond Hill, in an area of Kowloon with a high population density, you can find the serene Nan Lian Garden. It has only been opened for ten years but is an excellent example of a Chinese classical garden of the Tang Dynasty style complete with a pagoda, bridges, water features and gently swimming koi carp.

There is a small exhibition hall where you can see ornate carvings, a tea shop and a water garden.

A pleasant stroll around the garden (3.6 hectares) will take about half an hour and you can link your visit to the Chi Lin nunnery which is adjacent. There is a peaceful vegetarian restaurant in the gardens.

The Nunnery was founded in 1934 as a retreat for Buddhist nuns and rebuilt in the 1990s following the traditional Tang Dynasty architectural style. It was constructed from cypress wood, using interlocking joints and no nails whatsoever.

The main hall is currently the world's largest hand-made wooden building. The complex includes prayer halls, a library, a school, a pagoda a bell tower and drum tower. It is a working nunnery and parts are naturally out of bounds.

The atmosphere is very tranquil and peaceful - all the more significant considering the surrounding area.

The nunnery halls and the Chinese garden in front of the temple are open to the public.

Wong Tai Sin Temple

 Wong Tai Sin

 2327 8184

 Chuk Un, Wong Tai Sin, Kowloon

 Free

 07:00 – 17:00

 www1.siksikyuen.org.hk/en/wong-tai-sin-temple

One of the largest and perhaps most visited temples by locals and tourists is the Wong Tai Sin temple in North Kowloon. The temple is very easily reached from the MTR station which bears its name. In fact the whole area is named after Wong Tai Sin, a fourth century traveling monk.

Buddhism, Taoism and Confucianism coexist harmoniously and this is predominantly a temple with a famed collection of literature pertaining to that philosophy. The temple is invarlably busy and fortune tellers and soothsayers line the entrance. The main temple has been erected in the traditional Chinese way with grand red pillars and a golden roof with blue friezes. There is also a nine dragon wall - the name Kowloon means 'Nine dragons' and refers to the surrounding hills.

Many devotees at the temple come to seek a change of fortune. They light incense sticks and kneel before the altar to make a wish. They may also shake chim sticks in a small bamboo cask until one falls out. This numbered stick is exchanged for a paper bearing the same number and then taken to the soothsayer who will make predictions and write them on the paper. Sometimes the paper will be taken to several soothsayer booths for verification.

Fortune tellers in other booths offer palm and face reading to inform you what lies ahead. Several offer their services in English. A fee is charged.

Prayer flags, prayer wheels, calligraphy and other Buddhist related items are for sale and a great deal of activity can be observed at the temple complex.

Dining

Kowloon City itself contains several parallel shopping and dining streets. There is a Thai community here and the area is well-known for a number of inexpensive Thai restaurants.

Festival Walk, the large shopping mall at Kowloon Tong contains a variety of restaurant options including Chinese, Japanese, Italian, American and Thai. There is a food court on the top floor. Dan Ryan's on one the lower floors is an atmospheric American bar and grill serving good food and several varieties of chilled US beers.

Wong Chu Chun
Nearest MTR: *Mong Kok*
Address: *23 Tak Ku Ling Road, Kowloon City*
Opening Hours: *11:00 to 0:00*
Phone: *2716 6269*

This is one of the oldest and largest of the Thai restaurants in Kowloon City and it serves excellent food. The pineapple rice is delicious as are other favorites such as pad thai and various curry dishes.

Amaroni's Little Italy
Nearest MTR: *Kowloon Tong*
Address: *Shop 32, LG1, Festival Walk, 80 Tat Chee Avenue Kowloon Tong*
Opening Hours: *11:00 to 0:00*
Phone: *2265 8818*

Amaroni's in a popular Italian/American restaurant which aims to re-create a family atmosphere. It is a large and busy restaurant which serves very good nourishing food. The spaghetti with meatballs are especially good.

Billy Boozer
Nearest MTR: *Kowloon Tong*
Address: *Shop 20, Franki Center, 320 Junction Road, Kowloon Tong*
Opening Hours: *11:00 to 04:00*
Phone: *2339 0980*

This is an authentic British style pub which used to be a favorite of British soldiers pre-1997 but now attracts University students. It serves a variety of British beers as well as nourishing pub food. It stays open late and is known for its friendly staff.

Hotels

Harbour Grand Kowloon
Nearest MTR: *Hung Hom*
Address: *20, Tak Fung Street, Hung Hom*
Telephone: *2621 3188*
Website: *www.kowloon. harbourgrand.com*

This 555 room hotel is situated right on the Kowloon waterfront at Hung Hom to the east of TST. It has excellent views of the harbor and the Island skyline. Hung Hom MTR station is about 10 minutes away by minibus (less by taxi). There is a hotel shuttlebus which runs to TST every 20 minutes. The hotel has won recent Certificate of Excellence Awards. It has an outdoor pool, solarium, spa and fitness center

and scores highly for cleanliness, comfort and staff performance. Rooms are HK$1100

Regal Oriental
Nearest MTR: *Kowloon Tong*
Address: *30-38, Sa Po Road, Kowloon City*
Telephone: *2718 0333*
Website: *www. regalhotel.com/en*

This 494 room hotel is near the old airport (Kai Tak) which closed in 1998 - any building in the area which is more than four floors high would have been built since then. There is no MTR station within easy walking distance but the 25M minibus connects with Kowloon Tong. The hotel runs a shuttle bus to TST. The hotel scores well on cleanliness,

room comfort and value for money (HK$600).

Kowloon City Bridal Tea House
Nearest MTR: *Mong Kok*
Address: *14-18 Sung Wong Toi Road, To Kwa Wan*
Telephone: *2768 7211*
Website: *www.booking. com/hotel/hk/bridal- tea-house-tokwawan.en*

This modest 56 room hotel is a little out of the way but has direct bus connections with Star Ferry (5 and 5A). The rooms are small but clean, the staff are friendly and the hotel scores well for value. The site of the former airport is nearby and there is some construction noise. (HK$350).

D. Central/Admiralty Area

Central, the area once called Victoria and recognized as the capital of the territory, is essentially a business district where you will find many of the famous high rise office buildings, including headquarters of banks, financial corporations and multi-national companies.

The HSBC building and the Bank of China Tower are here but they are dwarfed by the 88 floor International Finance Center (IFC) on the waterfront.

Here you are well situated for The Peak Tram, The Botanical Gardens and the ferries to Kowloon and the Outlying Islands.

The Hong Kong business fraternity likes to play hard, as well as work hard, and close to Central you will find two areas that contain numerous bars and restaurants of all types. These are Lan Kwai Fong and SoHo (South of Hollywood Road).

Lan Kwai Fong is a popular area for bars, restaurants and nightlife. It is often frequented by fashionable expatriate office staff as well as tourists out for the evening. There are more than a hundred bars and restaurants crowded into the L shaped cobbled street of Lan Kwai Fong and the adjacent D'Aguilar Street, which also turns 90 degrees and results in almost a rectangle.

Various party events are organized by the Lan Kwai Fong Association to attract customers. The two streets are brightly decorated for Christmas, New Year's Eve, Chinese New Year, Valentine's Day and Halloween.

The atmosphere of an outdoor party is created on the cobbled streets to support the notion that Lan Kwai Fong is the place to go for a good time.

Attractions

The Hong Kong Police Museum

 Central (Exchange Square), then 15 bus

 Free

 2849 7019

 09:00 to 17:00. Closed all day Monday, and Tuesday morning.

 27 Coombe Road, The Peak

 www.police.gov.hk

This museum traces the history of the police force in the territory from the mid-19th century to the present day. It has four galleries - the Orientation Gallery, Triad Societies and Narcotics Gallery, Hong Kong Police Then and Now Gallery and a Thematic Exhibition Gallery.

Hong Kong Park

 Admiralty, Exit C   Free

 2521 5041   07:00 to 23:00

 19 Cotton Tree Drive, Central   www.lcsd.gov.hk/en/parks/hkp

This is a comparatively new, cleverly landscaped park close to the bustling Admiralty area near to Central. It was opened in 1991 and uses flowing water as a thematic link to connect different features. It covers an area of 8 hectares and includes Hong Kong's largest aviary, a greenhouse and an orchid area.

There is a garden plaza and a Tai Chi garden as well as sports facilities.

It is easily reached by escalator from the Pacific Place shopping mall which is adjacent to Admiralty MTR station.

The Museum of Tea Ware

 Admiralty, Exit C   Free

 2869 0690   09:00 to 18:00. Closed on Tuesday.

 10 Cotton Tree Drive, Admiralty   www.lcsd.gov.hk/CE/Museum/Arts/en

This museum is housed in Flagstaff House in Hong Kong Park. Built in 1846 this was the former home of the Commander of the British Forces and is the oldest colonial building in the territory. It is run by the Museum of Art and it traces tea culture through the ages and displays tea ware of all kinds.

Victoria Peak and the Peak Tram

 Central, Exit J2

 Single: HK$28. Return: HK$40

 2522 0922

 07:00 to 0:00

 Garden Road, Hong Kong

 www.thepeak.com.hk/en

Few people use the official name for the steep hill which dominates the center of Hong Kong Island and it is usually just referred to as 'The Peak'. It is arguably the number one tourist attraction and on most visitors' itineraries.

Part of the enjoyment of your visit is to ride up to the Peak (554m, 1818ft) on the historic Peak Tram. This funicular railway is an outstanding example of engineering skill from a bygone age, and was opened as long ago as 1888. It has been modernized and improved in the years since then but the experience of ascending and descending at a very steep angle (48 degrees) is memorable and very much as it was.

You can buy your ticket at the Peak Tram terminus which is about a 15 minute uphill walk from the HSBC building in Central. If you follow the signs for St John's Cathedral you can walk through the Cathedral grounds and take a pleasant short cut. You will need to cross busy Garden Road, however. An alternative to avoid the steep walk is to take the 15C shuttle bus from Star Ferry (HK side).

The Peak Tram does get extremely busy and if you want to avoid the crowds arrive early or go mid-week. The Tram only takes 120 passengers at once and you might have to queue for an hour or longer at busy times. The twenty minute ride is interesting as the tram by-passes 'stations' which were used in bygone times, and at the half way point lurches to pass the descending carriage.

At the top there are numerous attractions, souvenir shops and restaurants but the biggest treasures are of course, the amazing panoramic views to the North, above the Central skyscrapers, across the harbor to Kowloon, and beyond to the hills of the New Territories. Some people prefer to arrive in the late afternoon in order to witness twilight and the illumination of this photogenic city.

There are several viewpoint areas and, if you arrive in time and enjoy walking, you can hike the Peak Circle around the summit and also take in views to the south. This route starts near the old Peak Café in Lugard Road and follows a clockwise direction (allow 1 hour).

The Peak area has an interesting history and more than its share of luxurious houses and apartments. It was here that the colonials built their residences to escape the heat and humidity that plagued them lower down the hill. Today the real estate on the Peak remains numbingly expensive. If you want to pass by some of the residences scattered on the hill, consider taking a bus back down.

The bus terminus is well signposted and minibuses and double-deckers (15 and 15A) ply routes to and from convenient MTR stations.

Hong Kong Museum of Medical Sciences

 Central & take Mid-Levels escalator up

 HK$25 and HK$10 for concessions

 2549 5123

 10:00 to 17:00. Closed on Mondays, and Sunday mornings.

 2 Caine Road, Mid-Levels, Sheung Wan

 www.hkmms.org.hk/en

This museum was established in 1996, and is located in a renovated 3-story Edwardian-style building.

It is also referred to as the Old Pathological Institute and gives a fascinating insight into the development of medicine in the territory. There is an excellent exhibition about the human body.

The museum is surrounded by a pleasant open space in an area of numerous high rise residential buildings just off the Mid-levels escalator in Central.

Leave the escalator at Caine Road and turn right. The museum is about 200 meters on your right hand side at the junction with Ladder Street.

Hong Kong Zoological and Botanical Gardens

 See description for directions.

 $ Free

 2530 0154

 06:00 to 19:00 daily

 Albany Road, Central

 www.lcsd.gov.hk/en/parks/hkzbg

Directions: Central MTR Station. Exit at D2 and walk through Battery Path and the grounds of St. John's Cathedral. Turn right into Garden Road and follow signs (about 20 minutes).

This area on the northern lower slopes of Victoria Peak has been a refuge for busy office workers in nearby Central for decades. It was first cleared and planted as Hong Kong Botanical Gardens in 1871 and now has more than a thousand species of tropical and sub-tropical plants.

The zoological connection came later, and the name was changed in 1976 to reflect the growing commitment to animals. There are now 240 birds, 70 mammals and 20 reptiles in about 40 enclosures. There is also an aviary, bamboo garden, ornate fountain, education center and outdoor café.

The HKZBG covers an area of 5.6 hectares and its mammals include monkeys, gibbons, sloths and orangutans. If you want to avoid the steep 20 minute walk catch a number 12 or 13 bus from Central bus station.

The Mid-Levels escalator

 Central, Exit G.

 $ Free

 N/A

 06:00 to 0:00 daily - see description

 Jubilee Street, Central

 www.hongkongextras.com/_midlevels_escalators.html

Many high-rise housing developments, shops and restaurants are located on a number of streets which run parallel to Queen's Road in Central but are at increasingly higher levels - i.e. they are mid-level between the harbor and the summit of the Peak.

The area is called Mid-Levels, it is mainly an affluent one and you will find serviced apartments and residences whose rents reflect this.

To give easier access to residents and customers, the Mid-levels escalator was devised and installed in 1993. It is the longest outdoor covered escalator system in the world. Twenty connecting moving stairways and three walkways total 800 meters in length and climb 135 meters, from Queen's Road Central to Conduit Road.

The travel time to the top is 20 minutes. It goes downhill for the benefit of morning commuters from 06:00 until 10:00 then up the steep slope for the rest of the day, stopping operation at midnight. There are 14 entrances and exits.

From Central MTR, walk along Pedder Street and turn right into Queen's Road Central. The foot of the escalator is about 100m to your left.

Dining

Ce La Vi

Nearest MTR: *Central*
Address: *25/F California Tower, 36 D'Aguliar Street, Lan Kwai Fong*
Opening Hours: *12:00 to 15:00 and 18:00 to 23:00*
Phone: *3700 2300*

One of the favorites of young expatriates is 'Ce La Vi' which is a little different from the street side bars as it's on the 25th floor! Its Skybar has great views as well as a Jacuzzi and pool if you would like a dip between cocktails. The menu is a mixture of Japanese and Western dishes, the food is good but, needless to say, prices are not cheap here.

El Taco Loco

Nearest MTR: *Central*
Address: *9 Staunton Street, Mid- Levels*
Opening Hours: *12:00 to 22:00*
Phone: *2522 1252*

This is a Mexican Restaurant in the SoHo area very close to the Mid- Levels escalator. It serves a wide variety of well-prepared Mexican dishes, both vegetarian and meat based and is reasonably priced for the area.

There are numerous other good restaurants close to the escalator.

For Italian food try Al Dente also in in Staunton street (number 16). And there is a cozy British Pub (The Globe), at 45 Graham Street.

Many of the SoHo restaurants have lunchtime set menus, where you can get excellent value for food, although drinks can be expensive. Amble along Staunton Street and back along Elgin Street and you will have an extensive choice.

Jumbo Floating Restaurant

Nearest MTR: *Central, then taxi (20 minutes)*
Address: *Shum Wan Pier Drive, Aberdeen*
Opening Hours: *11:00 to 23:30*
Phone: *2553 9111*

Possibly one of the most famous restaurants in Hong Kong, The Jumbo Floating Restaurant and the adjacent Tai Pak Floating Restaurant (known collectively as Jumbo Kingdom) in the Aberdeen typhoon shelter are about 20 minutes by taxi from Central. They have been established for over 40 years.

The Jumbo cost millions of dollars to design and build and was styled in the fashion of an ancient Chinese imperial palace. Over the years, the restaurant has been valued by locals and tourists alike, and has become an iconic landmark of Hong Kong.

It serves traditional Cantonese cuisine and fresh seafood. Menus are in English as well as Chinese. It has had many distinguished guests over the years, including Queen Elizabeth II, David Bowie, Gwyneth Paltrow and Chow Yun Fat.

It can be quickly reached free of charge by shuttle boat from the nearby ferry pier. The restaurants get very busy but you can book well ahead by visiting the interactive website where you can also check the menu at jumbokingdom.com.

Hotels

Conrad Hotel
Nearest MTR: *Admiralty*
Address: *1, Pacific Place, 88 Queensway, Admiralty.*
Telephone: *2521 3838*
Website: *www. conradhotels3.hilton. com/en/hotels/hong-kong*

The entrance to the Conrad hotel is in the Pacific Place Mall. This is an award winning 5-star hotel that operates over 61 floors. Facilities include a fitness center, massage room, outdoor pool and unusually for Hong Kong hotels, a garden.

The afternoon tea buffet is excellent. It begins at 15:30 and it gets busy so you should arrive a little early. To do it justice, you should skip lunch and save your appetite!

There are 512 rooms and The Conrad gets great reviews for spaciousness of rooms, friendliness of staff and cleanliness. It isn't cheap however at HK$3000 per night.

The Bauhina
Nearest MTR: *Central*
Address: *119 Connaught Road, Central*
Telephone: *3426 3333*
Website: *www. thebauhinia.com.hk/ eng/our-hotels/central*

More modestly priced and considerably smaller is the Bauhina Hotel Central. This is a 42-room hotel in one of the main Central Streets and close to the MTR station. It has a fitness center and it scores well for staff friendliness, cleanliness and value at HK$950

Ibis Hong Kong Central
Nearest MTR: *Sheung Wan*
Address: *28 Des Voeux Road*
Telephone: *2252 2929*
Website: *www.ibis. com/en/hotel-7606-ibis-hong-kong-central-and-sheung-wan/index.shtml*

There are few budget hotels in the area but the Ibis Hong Kong Central is relatively modestly priced. It is a large (550 room) hotel situated to the west of Central, near to Sheung Wan MTR station. It has both Western and Chinese restaurants and gets good reviews for cleanliness, comfort and value at HK$650.

E. Wan Chai/Causeway Bay

This is an area of contrasts. The Hong Kong Convention and Exhibition Centre, the 78 story Central Plaza and the Hong Kong Centre for Performing Arts, where you will find several theaters, are all here.

A short bus or tram ride away is the very busy shopping options of Causeway Bay – a new, glitzy and very busy mall is called Times Square and it has its own MTR exit. You will find numerous eating and drinking establishments in the Food Court here.

There is also the 'red light district' of Wan Chai around Lockhart Road. This area was immortalized by Richard Mason in his 1957 novel 'The World of Suzie Wong', although reclamation has changed the location of the waterfront somewhat since then.

Lockhart Road contains ordinary bars, some British pubs including 'The Queen Victoria', as well as those which offer other services!

Attractions

Victoria Park

Tin Hau, Exit A2	Free
2890 5824	Open 24/7
Hing Fat Street, Causeway Bay	www.lcsd.gov.hk/en/parks/vp

The Park was named after the nineteenth century British Queen and her statue oversees one of the entrances. It is located close to the Causeway Bay waterfront and easily accessed from Tin Hau MTR station.

Victoria Park is the largest public park on Hong Kong Island (19 hectares). The Park is the venue for several annual events, both cultural and political.

It is the home to the Lunar New Year Fair, the Hong Kong Flower Show and lantern displays during the mid-Autumn Festival.

Victoria Park is perhaps best known internationally for the candlelight vigil which takes place annually on the night of June 4th. This is attended by thousands of Hong Kong people to remember the innocent victims of the 1989 Tiananmen Square Massacre by Chinese Communist troops in Beijing.

Victoria Park has children's playgrounds, tennis courts, bowling greens, football pitches and the oldest public swimming pool in Hong Kong (opened in 1957).

The tennis center court has seating capacity for nearly 4000 people and it hosts the Hong Kong Ladies Tennis Open.

The Noon Day Gun

 Causeway Bay, Exit D Free

 2508 1234 12:00 sharp daily

 Gloucester Road, Causeway Bay www.discoverhongkong.com/eng/see-do/culture-heritage/historical-sites/colonial/noon-day-gun.jsp

An interesting relic of colonial days is the ritual of the firing of a single shot over the harbor at the stroke of midday. A shell is fired above the water at the Causeway Bay Typhoon Shelter, near the Hong Kong Yacht Club every day.

This has been conscientiously observed since the early 1900s, apart from the period of Japanese occupation.

Often visiting dignitaries, local celebrities or philanthropists are invited to pull the lanyard to perform the ceremony.

The gun is owned and maintained by the very old local company Jardine Matheson and was possibly used as a way of synchronizing local time. The practice was immortalized in the famous song by Noel Coward 'Mad Dogs and Englishmen'.

You can watch the Noon Day Gun in operation by following the signs through underpass below the Excelsior Hotel (Causeway Bay MTR station, exit D).

Hong Kong Convention and Exhibition Centre and Golden Bauhinia Square

 Wan Chai

 2582 8888

 1 Expo Drive, Wan Chai

 Free for public areas. Check the website for individual exhibitions.

 07:30 for flag raising ceremony. Exhibition times will vary.

 www.hkcec.com/en/event-calendar

At the Wan Chai waterfront you will find the distinctive Hong Kong Convention and Exhibition Centre (HKCEC). This building was constructed on reclaimed land and completed in 1997, just in time for the historic July 1st handover. This is where the signing ceremony took place.

The roof of the HKCEC contains 40,000 m² of glass and aluminum, and represents a sea bird soaring in flight. It is best viewed from the TST waterfront opposite, or from Star Ferry. It is used for world class exhibitions and events, and includes two theaters. Check the website for events during your stay.

At Golden Bauhinia Square, beside the HKCEC, there is an impressive sculpture of a bauhinia flower, which is Hong Kong's emblem and appears on its flag. The bauhinia tree can be found all over the territory and its distinctive deep pink flowers bloom from November until March.

The sculpture was a gift from the Beijing government at the handover ceremony and every day this is the site of a ceremonial flag raising, which is particularly popular with visitors from the Mainland. It is performed by officers of the Hong Kong police in ceremonial uniform at 7:50am. The flag raising is accompanied by the playing of the Chinese national anthem.

On the first day of the month a Police rifle unit is in attendance, as well as a pipe band. The band gives a ten minute performance after the flag has been raised.

Dining

The American Peking
Nearest MTR: *Wan Chai*
Address: *20, Lockhart Road, Wan Chai*
Opening Hours: *11:30 to 23:30*
Phone: *2527 1000*

The American Peking is popular with locals and expatriates and serves delicious food. The crabmeat and sweetcorn soup is very good as are the sizzling prawns, onion cakes and duck.

The Coyote Bar and Grill
Nearest MTR: *Wan Chai*
Address: *114, Lockhart Road, Wan Chai*
Opening Hours: *12:00 to 02:00*
Phone: *2527 1000*

The Coyote serves good food and markets itself as 'Mexican with Attitude'. There is an extensive Mexican menu as well very good pizzas and Western Food. The restaurant is right in the heart of the Wan Chai nightlife area and can get very crowded. Live music is often on offer.

Hotels

The Excelsior
Nearest MTR: *Causeway Bay*
Address: *281 Gloucester Road, Causeway Bay*
Telephone: *2837 6840*
Website: *www.mandarinoriental.com/excelsior*

Overlooking the Causeway Bay waterfront, this is a well located hotel within minutes of Causeway Bay MTR station. It is a luxurious, famous hotel opened in 1973, with uniformed Cantonese/English speaking Sikh doormen.

It has 875 rooms, many of which have excellent harbor views. There are six restaurants, a fitness center and massage facilities. The Dickens Bar on the ground floor is a well-known meeting place for expatriate sports fans and it gets busy when big football or rugby matches are being televised. From the hotel you can walk to some of the busiest shopping streets in the territory. Rooms cost HK$1800.

The Cosmopolitan Hotel
Nearest MTR: *Causeway Bay*
Address: *387 Queens Road East, Wan Chai*
Telephone: *3552 1111*
Website: *www.cosmopolitanhotel.com.hk/en*

The Cosmopolitan Hotel is within easy reach of Happy Valley racecourse. There is no MTR here but there are trams and buses, and the hotel runs a shuttle bus to nearby centers. The hotel has a Western and Chinese restaurant and it scores well for cleanliness, staff performance and value. The 454 rooms recently underwent extensive renovations. Rooms start at about HK$800 per night.

The Walden Hotel
Nearest MTR: *Causeway Bay Exit C*
Address: *353 Hennessy Road, Causeway Bay*
Telephone: *8200 3308*
Website: *www.walden-hotel.com/home.htm*

The Walden Hotel has 54 rooms and is an 8 minute walk to Exit C of Causeway Bay MTR. It is reviewed as basic, and a little faded but gets good marks for cleanliness, hospitality and value at HK$450.

F. North Point/Quarry Bay

North Point is a bustling, mixed-use area of well-established shops, offices and hotels. Quarry Bay beside it is an alternative business hub to Central.

Although none of the main tourist attractions are in the immediate vicinity, the area is a convenient and generally less expensive option if you'd prefer to

be on Hong Kong Island.

It is just a few kilometers to the east of Central and easily accessed by MTR, bus and tram.

Attractions

The Hong Kong Museum for Coastal Defence

 Shau Kei Wan, Exit B2 + 15 minute walk

 HK$10 and HK$5 for concessions

 2569 1500

 10:00 to 18:00 in summer, and 10:00 to 17:00 in winter

 175, Tung Hei Road, Shau Kei Wan

 www.hk.coastaldefence.museum/en

This is a little off the beaten track but it is well worth a visit, especially for anyone interested in military history.

It is located at the coastal defence fort built in 1887 by the

British at a strategic point overlooking the eastern approach to the harbor.

Apart from exhibits from distant history, there is a fascinating gallery about the Japanese occupation, including

film footage. There are also some very moving enlarged photographs of individuals who were displaced by war.

Dining

Just five minutes' walk from exit A of Quarry Bay MTR station, you will find Tong Chong Street. This is a lively area containing many good bars and restaurants. Cuisines represented here include Cantonese, Taiwanese, Japanese, Turkish, French and American.

Enoteca

Nearest MTR: *Quarry Bay*
Address: *35, Tong Chong Street, Quarry Bay*
Opening Hours: *12:00 to 02:00*
Phone: *2744 6000*

Enoteca serves excellent tapas and Mediterranean food. You can eat al fresco here and it is a great place for Sunday brunch. In Quarry Bay the prices are cheaper and the bars a little less pretentious than Lan Kwai Fong.

On Sundays, Tong Chong Street hosts a food market which specializes in home grown, organic and unconventional food. Near to Tong Chong Street is the busy Taikoo Place, which is one of Hong Kong's newly developed business hubs. It contains the City Plaza shopping complex where you will find numerous restaurants and coffee shops. Food options here include Chinese, Japanese Korean, Thai, Italian and American.

Yue

Nearest MTR: *Fortress Hill*
Address: *1/F City Garden Hotel, 9 City Garden Road, North Point*
Opening Hours: *10:30 to 15:00 & 18:00 to 23:00*
Phone: *2806 4913*

Yue is one of Hong Kong's Michelin starred restaurants and is just five minutes from Fortress Hill MTR exit B. It specializes in dim sum and has won awards for no less than 5 of its signature dim sum dishes.

You would expect to pay high prices for food from a Michelin starred restaurant and indeed there are more than sixty of them in the territory. You can experience dim sum, however in more humble surroundings.

It is a long established Cantonese eating concept where small bite-sized food portions are served in small bamboo steamer baskets or on small plates. It is unique in the traditional way it is served in the older Chinese restaurants, where ready to eat delicacies are pushed around on trolleys in large and noisy restaurants. You choose at your table and a specific 'chop' associated with the dish is stamped onto your bill.

To get the maximum enjoyment from dim sum dining, you are advised to go with a local companion. The next best option is to ask at the entrance for an English speaking member of staff to help you, and explain the dishes. There are dim sum restaurants all over Hong Kong.

The Big Bite

Nearest MTR: *North Point*
Address: *G/F Kar Fu Building, 196 Java Road, North Point*
Opening Hours: *12:00 to 23:00*
Phone: *6979 9690*

Just five minutes' walk from Exit A4 of the MTR station, The Big Bite claims to serve the best burgers in Hong Kong. They are huge and served in fresh Kaiser Rolls. There is a wealth of other American dishes and refillable soft drinks at very reasonable prices.

Hotels

The Harbor Grand North Point

Nearest MTR: *Fortress Hill*
Address: *23 Oil Street, North Point*
Telephone: *2121 2688*
Website: *www.harbourgrand.com/en*

The Harbor Grand has 828 spacious rooms with panoramic views of the harbor or city, a large outdoor pool, fitness center, spa and steam room. There is a regular shuttle bus to Central, and there are Chinese, Japanese and Western dining options. Rooms are HK$1500.

The Newton Inn

Nearest MTR: *North Point*
Address: *88, Chun Yueng Street, North Point*
Telephone: *2130 3388*
Website: *www.newtoninn.com/en*

The Newton Inn is very close to North Point MTR station and within minutes of tram and bus stops. There are good views from the Harbor side of the hotel and the 317 rooms are spacious. There is a rooftop swimming pool, gym and sauna and choice of Western and Chinese restaurants. Rooms are competitively priced at HK$700.

The Homy Inn

Nearest MTR: *North Point*
Address: *275 Kings Road, North Point*
Telephone: *8100 0189*
Website: *www.homyinn.com.hk/en*

The Homy Inn is a 99 room hotel which gets very good reviews for cleanliness, friendliness of staff and value for money. It is in a good location near North Point MTR station, rooms start at HK$250.

G. Sha Tin

Sha Tin is a vibrant New Territories town with good connections to central areas of Hong Kong. It has extensive shopping facilities and a selection of restaurants of all cuisines.

There are pleasant riverside walks and here you are well situated for the Ten Thousand Buddhas monastery and lovely Sha Tin Park, which is a welcome oasis from the busy New Town Plaza nearby.

Attractions
Sha Tin Park

 Sha Tin, Exit A2

 2695 9253

 2, Yuen Wo Road, Sha Tin

 Free

 06:30 to 23:00 daily

 www.lcsd.gov.hk/en/parks/stp

In Sha Tin, which is described later in this chapter, there is a very attractive waterside park which contains an azalea garden, scented garden, bird conservation area and several children's playgrounds (including an adventure playground).

At the Artist's Corner, open at weekends and public holidays, local artists exhibit and sell their work.

Nearby is the Wedding Garden where couples gather for photographs.

From Sha Tin MTR station, walk through the busy shopping plaza towards the library and Town Hall. The river is ahead of you and the park is just to the right.

Hong Kong Railway Museum

 Tai Po Market, Exit A3

 2653 3455

 13 Shun Tak St., Tai Po Market, New Territories

 Free

 Monday and Wednesday – Sunday 10:00 to 18:00. Closed on Tuesday.

 www.heritagemuseum.gov.hk/en_US/web/hm/museums/railway.html

This museum is at Tai Po Market in the New Territories. It is not large but very interesting, especially to railway and history enthusiasts.

Displays outline the development of the railways in Hong Kong and their importance to the territory.

Exhibits include an historic station building, six carriages, a diesel engine and a narrow gauge steam locomotive.

Hong Kong Heritage Museum

 Sha Tin, Exit A2

 2180 8188

 1, Man Lam Road, Sha Tin

 HK$10 for a standard ticket and HK$5 for concessions

 Mon & Wed to Fri 10:00 to 18:00. Weekends/public holidays 10:00 to 19:00

 www.heritagemuseum.gov.hk/en

Another child-friendly museum is the Hong Kong Heritage Museum in Sha Tin. It is situated near the Shung Mun River and is a pleasant 15 minute walk from Sha Tin Town Hall in the direction of Tai Wai (to the right as you face the river).

This is a large museum with interesting cultural exhibits such as the history of Hong Kong cinema, a Bruce Lee memorial exhibition and a display of Cantonese opera. There is also a hands-on children's gallery and play area.

From Sha Tin Station walk through the shopping plaza to the Town Hall, turn right, walk along the Shing Mun River Promenade and follow the signs.

Sha Tin and the Temple of Ten Thousand Buddhas

 Sha Tin, Exit B

 Free, but donations are welcome

 2691 1067

 09:30 to 17:30 daily

 Tai Po Road, Sha Tin

 www.hongkongextras.com/_ten_thousand_buddhas_monastery.html

If you look at old maps, you will see that the Sha Tin waterfront has changed dramatically. Most of the town is built on reclaimed land either side of the now unnaturally straight Shing Mun River.

With a population of over 600,000 it is the largest and most easily accessed of the new towns. There are four bridges, and very pleasant waterfront walks on both sides of the river and an excellent park. A well-used cycle track is beside the river and nearby are bicycle shops where you can hire a bike for HK$50 to HK$100 a day.

The cycle track to Tai Po is about 11km long and it stays parallel to the water as it widens to form the Tolo Harbor. The track passes Sha Tin racecourse and the luxurious stables where the racehorses are housed.

In order to reach the Temple of Ten Thousand Buddhas, you need to navigate quite a steep climb up a path and concrete steps from Sha Tin MTR station. Just follow the signs to reach the path up to the Monastery complex. It is about a 20 minute moderately strenuous walk, but worth it, if for no other reason than to see the strange embalmed monk, covered in gold leaf, who founded the monastery and who presides there. From a glass case he peers out high above the sprawling metropolis far below.

There are in fact more than 12,000 statues - all different - which line the walls of the temples but there is also a pagoda, pavilions, meeting halls and several large, slightly sinister and gaudily painted statues.

Dining

Tai Yuen Dai Pai Dong
Nearest MTR: *Fo Tan*
Address: *Fo Tan Cooked Food Market, Shan Mei Street, Fo Tan, Sha Tin.*
Opening Hours: *18:00 to 03:00*
Phone: *2697 3656*

If you want to try some authentic inexpensive Cantonese cuisine, catch the 80M bus from outside Sha Tin Town Hall to Fo Tan. Get off the bus at Shan Mei Street, outside Fo Tan Post Office. Cross the road and to your left and right you will find a series of tarpaulin roofed dia pai dongs. One is called Tai Yuen.

The specialty here is roasted pigeon, but they also serve deep fried squid and seasonal vegetables.

There are five or six different establishments near to each other. You will sit on plastic stools and plastic covered toilet roll holders double as serviette dispensers, but the food is excellent.

City Art Restaurant
Nearest MTR: *Sha Tin*
Address: *2/F The Royal Park Hotel, 8 Pak Hok Ting Street, Sha Tin.*
Opening Hours: *12:00 to 15:00, 18:00 to 23:00*
Phone: *2694 3968*

The City Art restaurant serves excellent Chinese and Western dishes. The lunch buffet is very good value and will satisfy the hungriest diner. It is centrally located adjacent to New Town Plaza.

Jaspa's (Sai Kung)
Nearest MTR: *Ma On Shan, then 99 bus to Sai Kung. Or 299X bus from Sha Tin.*
Address: *13, Sha Tsui Path, Sai Kung, NT*
Opening Hours: *08:00 to 23:00*
Phone: *2792 6388*

Jaspa's in an excellent

Australian owned restaurant situated in the square in the middle of Sai Kung Town. As well as a wide variety of Western food, there are some superb Asian dishes available such as nasi goreng and Singapore noodles. Sing, the manager, is a well-known local personality who will always make you welcome.

It is also possible to hire the Jaspa's junk, where the restaurant will cater for your boat party which will set off for the day from Sai Kung Pier.

There is a direct bus connection between Sha Tin and Sai Kung (299X from the bus station) and the journey takes about 40 minutes. It is not necessary to retrace your steps as you can get a minibus from Sai Kung to either Choi Hung or Hang Hau MTR stations.

Hotels

The Hyatt Regency
Nearest MTR: *University*
Address: *18, Chak Cheung Street, Sha Tin.*
Telephone: *3723 1234*
Website: *www. hongkong.shatin.hyatt. com/en/hotel/home. html*

The Hyatt Regency is the first International class hotel in the New Territories and has only been opened for a short time. It is some distance from Sha Tin Center and next to University MTR station, two stops along the East Rail line.

There are choices of restaurants and bars, an outdoor pool, tennis courts and free shuttle bus services. It has 559 rooms and gets excellent reviews for cleanliness, staff attitude and value. You can get rooms from HK$1200.

The Regal Riverside
Nearest MTR: *Sha Tin*
Address: *34-36 Tai Chung Kiu Road, Sha Tin*
Telephone: *2649 7878*
Website: *www. regalhotel.com/regal-riverside-hotel/en/ home/home.html*

The Regal Riverside is conveniently situated alongside the Shing Mun River, on the far side of the town center, about a ten-minute walk from it. It is a large hotel with 1138 rooms, an outdoor pool, comfortable rooms and friendly staff. There are both Western and Chinese restaurants and convenience stores nearby. The river is tidal and at low tide it can get a little smelly. Rooms are very competitively priced at HK$600.

There are no budget hotels in Sha Tin, but an alternative New Territories town which is not too far from central areas is Tseun Wan. This is a busy industrial area but it does have some good hotels, many of which run shuttle buses to Tsim Sha Tsui.

The Panda Hotel (Tseun Wan)
Nearest MTR: *Tseun Wan*
Address: *3, Tsuen Wah Street, Tsuen Wan, N.T.*
Telephone: *2409 1111*
Website: *www. pandahotel.com.hk/en*

The Panda Hotel is close to Tsuen Wan MTR station and has excellent facilities, including a pool, fitness center and choice of restaurants. It is a large hotel with 911 rooms and it runs shuttle buses to TST.

It scores well for cleanliness and staff performance and is priced at HK$700.

H. Further Afield

In this chapter, we look at some of the lesser known destinations for those visitors who have the time and interest to experience a little more than the main attractions in order to better get to know this unparalleled destination.

The geography of the territory lends itself to hiking and there are four extensive trails which crisscross the hilly terrain. The British colonials were great hikers and the two longest trails have been named after governors who enjoyed the outdoors. These trails are covered in this section.

Attractions

Inspiration Lake

 Hong Kong Disneyland

 Free

 3550 3388

 09:00 to 19:00 daily.

 Hong Kong Disneyland Resort, Lantau Island

 www.hongkongdisneyland.com/destinations/inspiration-lake-recreation-centre

Within a fifteen minute walk of Disneyland is Inspiration Lake, a large artificial lake and surrounding recreation area built by the Hong Kong government.

The facilities here include a boating center, arboretum, 1500 meter jogging trail, bicycle rental shop, exercise areas and children's playground.

The lake itself has water cascades, aquatic plants and a jet which can shoot water 18 meters high.

Hong Kong Disneyland Resort

 Hong Kong Disneyland

 3550 3388

 Hong Kong Disneyland Resort, Lantau Island

 One Day - HK$539 for adults, HK$385 for children & HK$100 for seniors

 10:30 to 20:00 daily. Later closings at peak times.

 www.hongkongdisneyland.com/eng

Opened in September 2005 at Penny's Bay on Lantau Island just off the freeway to the airport, this theme park has similar attractions to other Disneyland resorts. It has seven themed areas – Main Street USA, Fantasyland, Adventureland, Tomorrowland, Grizzly Gulch, Mystic Point and Toy Story Land. There is a daily parade and a nighttime firework display, as well as numerous dining and shopping outlets.

Disneyland is a world famous destination for children and adults alike, and the numerous exhibits have all been carefully planned for optimum enjoyment. The rides and parades are lavish, exciting and spectacular.

Most of the staff speak Cantonese, English and Mandarin, announcements are in those three languages. Maps and guides are available in several other languages also.

Hong Kong Disneyland has a daily capacity of 34,000 visitors and it receives close to five million visitors annually. It has its own MTR station which is easily and quickly accessed from Sunny Bay and can be reached from Central in about 35 minutes. Buses also run to the resort from all over the territory. For your easiest route, as well as special events, check the website.

You really should set aside the whole day to see the wealth of attractions and to get value for your admission fee.

There are two hotels in the Park complex, Disney's Hollywood Hotel and the Hong Kong Disneyland Hotel.

The Big Buddha

 Tung Chung + Cable Car

 Single: HK$130, Return: HK$185 on cable car.

 2985 5248

 10:00 to 18:00 on weekdays, 09:00 to 18:30 on weekends and public holidays

 Po Lin Monastery, Ngong Ping, Lantau Island

 www.np360.com.hk/eng

The Big Buddha at Ngong Ping on Lantau island, or to give it its correct name Tian Tan Buddha should be a 'must see' on your itinerary.

Although you can get to it by a longer route (ferry from the Central Pier to Mui Wo and then the winding bus), it would be a pity to miss the fabulous cable car ride. The cable car, opened in September 2006, was built solely to give easy access to the Buddha, and it can get very busy, especially at weekends. It begins at the new town of Tung Chung, near the airport, and is well signposted from the MTR station.

It isn't cheap but if you choose a clear day the views are outstanding. The cable car ride takes about 25 minutes.

Each car can carry 10 seated passengers and has room for 7 standing. The system can transport up to 3000 people per hour. Special cars have been adapted for wheelchairs.

The area around the cable car exit at the end of your ride is rather over-commercialized, and you will find souvenir shops and restaurants. It is a short stroll to the foot of the steps and a reasonably steep ascent (268 steps) to the top of the statue. You should take some water,

especially on a hot day.

The bronze Buddha itself is the largest seated replica of the deity in the world and it dominates the surrounding landscape, giving you great photo opportunities. You can enter a circular room beneath the statue and learn about its construction and funding.

The Po Lin monastery which is a few minutes' walk from the foot of steps, has been located at Ngong Ping for many years and is worth a visit in its own right. It is a working monastery and you can even buy an inexpensive and nourishing vegetarian meal here.

Ocean Park

 Admiralty, Exit B + Bus 629 (20 minutes)

 HK$385 for adults and HK$193 for children between 3 and 11 years.

 3923 2323

 10:00 until 18:00. May stay open later during peak periods.

 Ocean Park, Shouson Hill, Hong Kong

 www.oceanpark.com.hk/en

Ocean Park on the south side of Hong Kong Island and opened in 1977. It is very spread out and covers 91.5 hectares on two levels. The upper level can be accessed by a 1.5 km cable car from the waterfront main entrance.

Ocean Park is an animal park, marine mammal park, oceanarium and amusement park (with four roller coasters) and boasts more than 80 attractions and rides. It received 7.8 million visitors in 2014, making it the thirteenth most visited theme park in the world and the largest in Asia. Half of all the visitors come from Mainland China.

The Park is sub-divided into 8 zones. These are Amazing Asian Animals, Aqua City, Whiskers Harbor, Marine World, Polar Adventure, Adventure Land, Thrill Mountain and The Rainforest.

Ocean Park does important educational work and scientific research to help the preservation of Ocean life. There are various animal encounters including excellent sea lion and bird shows. It has had some success in breeding rare shark species, bottlenose dolphins, pygmy marmosets, anacondas and other endangered animals.

The Park has more than 12,000 animals in total. Endangered birds and butterflies are also bred successfully.

You can take the dedicated shuttle bus from Admiralty but other public buses run to the waterfront entrance from different origins and details of these can be found by visiting the website.

The Wilson Trail

 See description.　　 Free

 N/A　　 Daylight hours.

 Stanley Gap Road, Stanley, Hong Kong　　 www.hiking.gov.hk/eng/longtrail/wtrail/wtrail.htm

A hiking trail was established in 1996 and was named for the last but one governor of Hong Kong, Sir David Wilson.

It has ten stages and goes from south to north, starting at Stanley on the south side of Hong Kong Island and finishing at Nam Chung in the north east New Territories.

The Wilson Trail is 78km long and you have to take the MTR to cross the harbor. There are several points where hiking trails cross others, and the stages are at various levels of difficulty but their beginnings can be accessed by public transport.

For the start go to Central MTR Station, take Exit A to Exchange Square Bus station and take double decker 6X to Stanley.

The Dragon's Back Trail

 See description.

 9168 4803

 Wan Cham Shan, Hong Kong

 Free

 Daylight hours.

 Website: www.walkhongkong.com/ guidedhikeshongkong/dragonsbackhike.html

This hike was selected by Time Asia as the best urban hiking trail in the South East Asian region.

It is easily accessible and it does give outstanding views of urban landscapes, hillsides, coast and offshore islands. It is 8.5km from start to finish and includes some steep climbs, often on steps.

Depending on your speed it will take between 3 and 4 hours and you can have a refreshing swim at Big Wave Bay at the hike's end.

There is little shade on the walk so you should take a hat, water and sunscreen.

To begin take the MTR to Shau Kei Wan MTR station and exit at A3. You then catch bus number 9 towards Shek O and get off at Cape Collinson Road.

There is a steep set of steps just past the crematorium, which is the start of the hike. The trail is well marked.

The MacLehose Trail

 See description.　　 Free

 N/A　　 Daylight hours.

 Sai Kung Country Park, New Territories　　 www.hiking.gov.hk/eng/longtrail/mtrail/mtrail.htm

Sir Murray MacLehose, the governor responsible for the introduction of the Independent Commission Against Corruption, was a great lover of open spaces. During his time in office (1971-1982) he came to appreciate the need to conserve the countryside. Under his guidance, 21 country parks were designated, in effect protecting about 40% of the natural landscape.

His name is remembered through the 100km MacLehose Trail which he instigated. The trail crosses the New Territories and parts of Kowloon from east to west. It consists of 10 stages of varying lengths and difficulties and climbs from sea level to 957m (3140ft). It traverses some amazing landscapes, both natural and man-made including reservoirs, rugged peaks and remote valleys. It provides amazing views from sprawling urban developments to sheltered fishing coves, and you may even encounter a water buffalo or two!

Along the whole trail, after each 500 meters, there is a numbered distance post. Most of the ten stages begin and end at a place where you can get easy access to public transport. Look for the distinctive logo of a rucksack wearing hiker to ensure you are on the right track.

The MacLehose Trail is well used at weekends but not so much that you will not get long stretches to yourself. It does get significantly busier in the months leading to the annual Oxfam 'Trailwalker' charity event every November. This is when teams of four have up to 48 hours to complete the whole route. At the highest level, teams are very competitive, but the goal of others is just to finish within the time limit. The event attracts local groups as well as competitors from overseas. In late summer and early autumn, you will probably see teams in training, some even running!

Individual stages of the trail are mostly less than 12km and they are on well-worn, if sometimes steep, tracks. The stages vary in how challenging they are, and you do need a reasonable level of fitness. Before hiking on any of the trails you should inform someone of your route, pack plenty of water, hot and wet weather protection, suitable footwear and a mobile phone. For details and access points of the different stages, visit the government hiking website above.

For Stage One go to Choi Hung MTR, exit at C and catch the 1A minibus to Sai Kung. From Sai Kung bus station take double decker 94, alight at Pak Tam Chung and walk ten minutes to the start of the trail.

Kowloon Reservoirs and the Macaque monkeys

Very close to the sprawling urban developments of Kowloon, you will find the Kowloon Reservoirs and the Kam Sham Country Park.

Here there is a colony of rhesus macaque monkeys who have perfected the art of survival, and live very close to human habitation. They were not originally from the area and their ancestors were probably pets which were set free in the 1920s.

Estimates put the number of wild monkeys in Hong Kong at 2,100, of which 1,800 have adapted to their surroundings at Kam Sham.

From the bus stop in Nathan Road outside Kowloon Central Post Office near Yau Ma Tei MTR station, catch the number 81 bus. This bus goes along the Tai Po Road, which is an alternative route to Tai Wai and Sha Tin, avoiding the often congested Lion Rock Tunnel.

Get off the bus at Golden Pond Road and turn left into this road and cross the bridge over the stream which flows from one of the reservoirs. Continue along this road (in the direction of the MacLehose trail stage 6), and you are sure to see families of monkeys.

Monkeys gather along the quiet road and raid the litter bins for scraps left by picnickers. The females and young are fascinating to watch as they acrobatically leap through the trees, but beware of the mature males.

These are wild animals who show no fear of humans. They are unlikely to attack you unless you threaten them but neither will they move out of your way. The males are protective of their troupe and they will stare daggers if you linger in their territory. Do not carry visible food, or they will unceremoniously steal it from you.

The Agriculture and Fisheries department advise people not to feed these animals and you can be fined if you do so. They can become reliant on human food and may lose their skills of scavenging and gathering fruits and insects and may also be a danger to traffic. You might want to carry a hiking stick, purely as a precaution.

The Shing Mun Redoubt

If you continue along Golden Pond Road and up to MacLehose Stage 6, you will pass the Shing Mun Redoubt which was part of the 'Gin Drinker's Line' a system of observation towers and tunnels constructed to defend Hong Kong from the Japanese invasion in the Second World War.

The British soldiers who dug them in the late 1930s kept their sense of humor and you can clearly see the names on the tunnel entrances in honor of fashionable London Streets. 'Shaftesbury Avenue' for example connects with 'Regent Street' and 'Charing Cross'.

The defence line proved to be ineffective and the Japanese were only held at bay for two days.

MacLehose Stage Six is one of the shortest stages and you will descend to the Shing Mun country park where you can easily catch a minibus to Tseun Wan MTR station.

Tai Po Kau Nature Reserve

 Tai Po, then 72A bus   Free

 2708 8885   Daylight hours.

 Old Tai Po Road, Tai Po Kau, New Territories   www.afcd.gov.hk/english

This is a very pleasant country park on the outskirts of Tai Po which is maintained by the Agriculture, Fisheries and Conservation Department. There are four color coded circular walks through woodland, bamboo groves and across bubbling streams. It's a favorite haunt for bird watchers and hikers and is easily reached by public transportation.

You will pass the Chinese University on your right and the Nature Reserve is on the left, up a steep path. Ask the driver to tell you when to get off the bus, as it is easy to pass. When you have finished your hike you can carry on to Tai Po MTR or retrace your steps to Tai Wai.

The Hong Kong Wetland Park

 Tin Shui Wai

 3152 2666

 Wetland Park Road, Tin Shui Wai

 HK$30 and HK$15 for concessions

 10:00 to 17:00. Closed on Tuesdays.

 www.wetlandpark.gov.hk/en/

This is a delightful, natural area near to the Chinese border which has been preserved as an unspoiled conservation zone.

It covers an area of 60 hectares and includes mangroves, fishponds, reed beds, three bird hides, wetlands board walks and exhibition galleries.

It also contains a specially built enclosure and its occupant, Pui Pui - the saltwater crocodile - who mysteriously appeared in a Yuen Long river in November 2003.

Despite sightings and intense publicity, he successfully evaded capture until the following June, making light of the efforts of an expert crocodile catcher flown especially from Australia.

Patient bird watchers may be rewarded at the Wetland Park by sightings of spoonbills, herons, egrets, avocets and curlews.

Hong Kong Wetland Park can be reached by Light Rail Transit 705 to the stop which bears its name, from Tin Shui Wai MTR station on the West Rail line.

Lions Nature Education Centre

 Tseun Kwan O +
792M Bus

 Free

 2792 2234

 09:30 to 19:00. Closed on Tuesdays.

 Hiram's Highway East,
Sai Kung

 www.afcd.gov.hk/english/country/cou_
con/cou_con.html

This is a very pleasant oasis near to Sai Kung. It was created by the Lions Club and is now run by the Agriculture, Fisheries and Conservation Department.

The Centre is well-used by day trippers and school groups from Kowloon to get a taste of the countryside.

Inside the landscaped gardens is an arboretum, a vegetable garden, a dragonfly pond and displays of different plants and grasses found in Hong Kong.

There is a small museum with exhibitions of bird and animal life. There is also a geological exhibition describing different local rocks, and a short nature trek. A newly renovated café is run by hearing impaired staff.

The 92 bus from Diamond Hill, and the 792M stop outside the Lions Nature Education Centre. From here it is a short bus ride or fifteen minute walk to the town of Sai Kung.

Sai Kung

Thirty years ago Sai Kung, in the east of the New Territories, was a sleepy fishing village. Now it is a bustling waterside town with shops, restaurants and parks. It embraces its role as a center for hiking and boating in the area, and it is adjacent to the Sai Kung Country Park.

Sai Kung still retains a lot of its small town charm, but be wary of arriving at the weekend, especially when the weather is fine. Many people come out from busy Kowloon and it is also on the itinerary of several Mainland tour companies.

The old town is a labyrinth of narrow streets with shops and houses just meters from each other. There are all sorts of small businesses ranging from dry goods, to fruit and vegetables and curios.

There is a Tin Hau temple and an unusual line of elevated bells which run from the temple and mark where the waterline used to be before reclamation. The promenade provides a pleasant walk of about 2km passing numerous very busy sea food restaurants. These have many of their menu items on display, still swimming in large tanks beside them!

From the elevated pier you can see fisher folk selling their newly caught sea life from small boats. They pass the bagged sea food up to customers in a net on a long pole, and cash is dropped into the net. If you are squeamish you might not wish to see the live fish being de-scaled and gutted just before sale – sometimes still wriggling!

There are numerous options for boat trips from the waterfront and a one hour trip to see some outlying islands and interesting volcanic rock formations costs about HK$200. There are several European bars and restaurants around the square in the center of town, and many Westerners live in the surrounding villages. Sai Kung homes are mainly low rise, and may even have gardens - a rarity for Hongkongers.

There is no MTR in Sai Kung but you can catch a 1A green minibus from Choi Hung MTR (Exit C) or a 101M green minibus from the bus station at Hang Hau MTR. Both journeys take about 25 minutes and cost around HK$9. There is also a red minibus to Sai Kung from a stop in Dundas Street near Yau Ma Tei MTR in Kowloon. The fare is HK$16 and the trip takes about 40 minutes.

The Outlying Islands

Hong Kong has many outlying islands. The three largest and most populated are Lantau, Cheung Chau and Lamma. Ferries are frequent and easily accessible from the Outlying Island Ferry Piers in Central, which are adjacent to the Star Ferry Pier. Each of these three islands is interesting and worth visiting.

Ferries to Lantau and Cheung Chau are operated by New World First Ferry. Their website is www.nwff.com.hk. The ferry to Lamma is operated by Hong Kong and Kowloon Ferry Holdings Limited whose website is www.hkkf.com.hk.

Lantau
Lantau is the largest of the Outlying Islands with an area of 147.2km^2 (56.8mi^2). In comparison Hong Kong Island is 80.4km^2 (30mi^2).

Twenty years ago, Lantau had a very sparse population. Extensive reclamation, the construction of the new airport on its North side and the accompanying new town of Tung Chung have completely transformed that side of the island. South Lantau however, has remained largely unaltered.

A day trip to the small villages and beaches or some secluded hikes in the Lantau hills will make you wonder whether you are still in Hong Kong. You will need the Mui Wo ferry from the Central Piers and the journey takes about an hour.

Mui Wo is a small village with a few restaurants, bicycle hire shops and a pleasant beach. If you catch the bus from the ferry terminus to Tong Fuk or Cheung Sha you will find some of the best beaches in the territory.

Tai O village is very much an outpost of Hong Kong. It is famous for its wooden stilt houses built above the creek, and the local shrimp paste. It also has an interesting history connected with smuggling.

You can find some good sea food restaurants here and buses run back to the Mui Wo ferry every hour - don't forget to check the timetable.

If you visit the Nong Ping monastery you need not retrace your steps and you can return via the cable car to Tung Chung.

Cheung Chau

Cheung Chau is also about an hour away (or less by fast ferry).

This is a surprisingly busy fishing and tourist island in the shape of a bone. No cars are allowed on the island but small motorized tuk-tuks trundle to and fro, carrying building materials or the stock for shops.

All along the waterfront are seafood restaurants but as you get away from the main street there is an ice making factory and interesting chandlers where you can watch fishing boats being repaired. Look out for the narrow fire engines and ambulances, specially adapted for the Cheung Chau roads.

There is a sandy beach with changing facilities on the far side of the island (just 10 minutes from the ferry pier), near to the Warwick Hotel.

The 'afternoon beach' just along the coast was named by colonials for the shade it gives. The beach is good for swimming and water sports and it was here that HK's only Olympic gold medalist Lee Lai Shan trained before she took the windsurfing gold medal at the Atlanta Olympics.

Cheung Chau is also home of the annual bun festival.

Lamma

Lamma is the closest of the larger islands, and it has a permanent population of just over 6000.

The ferry from Central takes about 20 minutes, and there is also a ferry to and from Aberdeen on the south of Hong Kong Island.

Apart from an unsightly power station, it is a good place for hiking. There are pleasant beaches and swimming areas.

You can do a 7km linear hike here from Yung Shue Wan on one side of the island to Sok Kwu Wan on the other. Ferries run to both villages.

Lamma has several restaurants which specialize in sea food and is also home to Hong Kong's first (and so far, only) wind turbine.

Kat Hing Wai Walled Village

 Tai Po Market + 69K bus

 Free, but a donation for the village upkeep is expected.

 N/A

 Daylight hours.

 Kam Tin, Yuen Long, New Territories

 www.bit.ly/kathingwai

If you are interested in history, you should visit one of the walled villages that still remain in pockets of the New Territories, in order to get a feel of what life was like before the British arrived.

One of the best preserved examples is the walled village of Kat Hing Wai, near the town of Kam Tin which can be accessed by bus 54 from Yuen Long Town Centre, or 64K from Tai Po Market MTR Station on the East Rail.

The village was constructed nearly 400 years ago during the Ming dynasty. It was built by the Tang clan to protect its members from bandits, rival clans and even tigers which once roamed freely.

The village is brick built and rectangular in shape with a rather neglected moat outside. The Iron gates have an interesting history being once confiscated by the British and later returned.

Although many of the houses inside the village have been modernized, the walls and gates are original and you can freely wander the narrow streets. The 400 or so residents are all members of the ancient Tang clan and can trace their ancestry back four centuries.

At the village, you are likely to be good humoredly accosted by several elderly ladies who sit by the gate. They are uniquely dressed in traditional 'Punti' black fringed straw hats. They are inviting you to take their photographs and will be happy for you to snap away for HK$20.

Hong Kong Beaches

You might not automatically think of Hong Kong as being a beach destination, but there are 38 of them in use. These are managed by the Leisure and Cultural Services Department.

Each one of these beaches has had shark prevention nets installed, after few incidents in the early1990s.

Ten of these beaches are on the South side of Hong Kong Island, nine are in the Outlying islands, thirteen are in the West of the New Territories (Tuen Mun and Tseun Wan districts) and six are in the East (Sai Kung district).

Hong Kong beaches have all been 'gazetted' which means they have passed minimum standards in the Government Gazette as bathing beaches. They all have toilets, showers, changing rooms and first aid posts. They are supervised by lifeguards between the months of April and October.

The water quality at each of the beaches is regularly tested and categorized as good, fair or poor. The results are displayed at the beaches and also published and regularly up dated on the interactive web site of the Environmental Protection Department at www.beachwq.gov. hk/en/

Although the waters of the South China Sea are not the clearest and you won't see much through a snorkel, you can still enjoy safe swimming in reasonably clean seas.

There are anchored rafts that you can swim to, and most of the gazetted beaches are sandy. In our opinion, two of the best Hong Kong beaches are Stanley Main Beach and Trio Beach near Sai Kung.

Shopping

Hong Kong is world famous for its shopping for all budgets - from the small family run lock-up to the extravagant designer store. Most large stores open daily, usually from 10:30am to 9:00pm or 10:00pm.

Luxury Retailers

Along Canton Road in Tsim Sha Tsui, and in Queens Road and Des Voeux Road in Central you will find some of the most up-market stores in the world.

Here, and in the air conditioned shopping malls of IFC, Pacific Place, Times Square, Ocean Terminal and Prince's Building, world famous fashionable icons rub shoulders with each other – brands such as Giorgio Armani, Louis Vuitton, Burberry, Gucci, Prada, Dolce and Gabbana, Cartier and others.

Affluent locals, well-heeled mainland Chinese and International jet-setters wave their credit cards without a moment's hesitation to purchase luxury goods here.

Many of these shops are image conscious and prefer not to let themselves get too crowded and at times you might see queues of people waiting outside to enter (especially at the Canton Road branches).

Author's Insight: One day I observed the queue and noticed that the patient line seemed to consist mainly of humbly and inexpensively dressed people. A local friend enlightened me. Some of the shoppers are so wealthy that they employ 'professional queue standers' to wait in the line while they sip tea or cocktails at one of the nearby Five Star Hotels. When the entry turn is imminent, a quick mobile call will allow the boss to stroll over and take his/her place near the front!

Department Stores

Hong Kong also has its share of locally owned department stores. One of the most exclusive is Lane Crawford, which has a history going back to 1850 when it opened as a ship's chandlers. Now it is dominated by designer clothes, handbags, shoes and home ware. The largest two of the four Lane Crawford stores are in the IFC Mall in Central and at Harbor City in Tsim Sha Tsui.

Shanghai Tang is another local store with several branches, now also overseas. It tries to capture the spirit of 1920s Shanghai by selling traditional styles such as cheongsam dresses and knot button jackets. Their logo appears on elaborate photograph frames, writing cases and more. The flagship store is in Pedder Street, Central.

Hong Kong is fascinated by all things Japanese and there is a large Japanese department store in Causeway Bay called Sogo. It features 12 floors and departments such as fashion, homeware, cosmetics and electronics. As well as international brands, the store sells Japanese goods that are not always found elsewhere in the territory.

Of the British department stores, Harvey Nichols is perhaps the most up market. It has a large store at Pacific Place in Admiralty and sells men's and women's clothing, cosmetics and jewelry. Many of the items sold are unique to Harvey Nichols and their exclusivity is reflected in the prices.

Famous British company Marks and Spencer has several branches around the territory including large outlets in Central and Tsim Sha Tsui. As well as clothing, cosmetics and accessories, it has a high reputation for its food and some stores sell food alone. One of these can be found near the foot of the Mid–Levels escalator in Queens Road Central.

Some department stores focus on Chinese goods and one of the most famous is Yue Hwa on the junction of Nathan and Jordan Roads. There is a Chinese medicine department and others focused on fine silks, embroidery, wooden carvings and clay pots. This is a good starting point if you want to take something home with a Chinese theme.

Other large shopping malls include Telford Gardens in Kowloon Bay, Festival Walk in Kowloon Tong and New Town Plaza in Sha Tin.

These malls contain food outlets, coffee shops and often cinemas and their air-conditioned comfort provides a welcome refuge from the outside heat and humidity during the summer months.

Many of the malls contain familiar shops that you can find all over the world - Body Shop, Toys R Us, Zara, Guess, Mango, Swatch, etc. There are also locally established business chains which appear all over the territory. These include Broadway and Fortress for electronic devices, Watsons and Mannings for pharmaceuticals and bathroom supplies, Page One for books, magazines and cards and Bonjour for perfumes and cosmetics. Most large shopping malls are close to MTR stations.

There are many thousands of small businesses operating at street level in tiny shops. When you wander the streets of the urban areas. you might notice that the sale of some retailed goods are gathered together. Fa Yuen Street, after you cross Mong Kok Road away from the street market specializes in sports shoes, Tung Choi Street North is the street of tropical fish. Wing Lok Street in Sheung Wan sells dried sea food and tonic ingredients.

Street Markets

There are numerous local street markets in the territory and if you wander the streets of the urban areas you are sure to stumble across some of them. They are great places for people-watching and taking in the sights and sounds of the locals going about their daily shopping. Many Hongkongers insist on food shopping every day to ensure they get the freshest ingredients.

Some of the street markets are well known and will certainly be worth a visit if you are looking for souvenirs of your visit.

Although you can bargain a little for non-consumable goods, prices in the markets are usually reasonable, and unless you are quoted an exorbitant rate, you are only likely to get a few dollars discount.

The market traders have a living to make and there is little to be gained by trying to beat them down to the last dollar. Remember the cost of the item at home, and if it is a bargain to you, it is a genuine bargain even if your friend bought it for a few dollars less.

Stanley Market

Stanley Market is perhaps the best known and is on most tourists' itinerary. Here you will find a whole range of Hong Kong souvenirs, clothing, bags, scarves, ties, elaborate chopsticks and other items that have been developed for the tourist market. You will also rub shoulders with visitors from all over the world.

The market is in covered alleys near the center of the town, which was once a thriving fishing port. Stanley Main Beach is good for swimming on a warm day, and there are many bars and restaurants nearby.

While in Stanley, if you look inside the Tin Hau temple near the waterfront you can see the skin (now looking decidedly faded and shabby) of the last tiger shot in Hong Kong in 1942.

Further along the waterfront near to a jetty in the restaurant area is Murray House, an old colonial building which houses a maritime museum and restaurants. Believe it or not, this building was once sited in Central and was dismantled stone by stone in 1982 and rebuilt exactly as it was in its new location several years later.

Allow up to two hours to do the market justice, longer if you intend to eat and explore.

There is no MTR link to the south side of Hong Kong but Stanley is served by frequent double decker buses from Central Bus Station (6, 6X).

The Ladies Market.
This is an open air street market in Tung Choi Street in the very busy Mong Kok area of Kowloon. It is a bustling market which also sells Hong Kong souvenirs as well as bags, tee shirts, watches, jewelry and gadgets.

Go to Mong Kok MTR station and leave at exit E2. The market is very close to the MTR and clearly signposted.

There is a row of inexpensive local restaurants with English menus on the left as you near the end of the market. If you don't want to retrace your steps turn right here (Dundas Street), then left at busy Nathan Road. Yau Ma Tei MTR station is a few minutes' walk ahead of you.

Fa Yuen Street
This is very good for wool, household items and inexpensive ladies' and men's clothing. As well as the street stalls, there are numerous small clothing and houseware outlets on either side of the street. Go to Prince Edward MTR and leave at exit B2.

Western Market
This is a covered market housed in a newly refurbished Edwardian building and it specializes in cloth and material which is available by the meter. There is an interesting model shop on the ground floor which sells replicas of Hong Kong transportation vehicles. One of the termini of the 'ding-ding' trams is Western Market, alternatively go to Sheung Wan MTR station and leave at exit B.

Cat Street
This is an outdoor market alongside shops and it specializes in Chinese antiques, curios, medals, coins, postcards and other second hand items. You will be able to buy a copy of Chairman Mao's little red book and even a fifties alarm clock with his portrait on the face. Take the Mid–Levels escalator as far as Hollywood Road, turn right and follow the tourist signs until you reach the market which is in Upper Lascar Street.

Temple Street Night Market
This is our personal favorite for, although it may not be the best for bargains, it has so much more to offer - especially for people-watchers.

As well as the inevitable stalls, selling an assortment of souvenirs, appliances and miscellaneous electronic and household items, it has some excellent inexpensive *dai pai dong* eating establishments as well as other surprises. It sets up just before dusk and continues until late at night.

The market is in the street named after the Tin Hau temple which is roughly half way along it. The small open space around the temple attracts small groups of locals playing cards or Chinese chess and they are interesting to observe.

Nearby you will pass some karaoke parlors. These are small shops with portraits of female singers outside. You will possibly hear some local 'Canto-pop' tunes being performed less than perfectly. In fact, for a few dollars, anyone can take the microphone with the lady singer of their choice, while their friends listen and have a drink or two.

Around the temple area also you will find numerous fortune tellers in small booths, intently examining faces or hands. Some advertise their services in English. If you are lucky you might see the fortune teller with his little bird. When prompted the bird will hop along an array of small cards to pick out one with his beak. The proprietor will then interpret the chosen card for you.

Alongside the fortune tellers are the music booths where small groups play Chinese instruments to accompany Cantonese opera performers. You can pay a few dollars to get a seat within the booth for a closer view! You will see life at Temple Street.

Go to Jordan MTR exit A, turn right into Jordan Road and right again into Temple Street. At the far end of the market you will be at the next MTR station Yau Ma Tei.

Flower Market
Hong Kong people love flowers and enjoy giving and receiving them. If you visit the aptly named Flower Market Street you will see a whole street of florists selling a wide variety of flowers and growing plants. The market operates from the early morning and gets really busy in the run up period to Chinese New Year when cherry blossom and kumquat plants are particularly in demand. If you want some flowers to take to a friend, it is here you will get the best bargains. Use Prince Edward MTR Exit B1 and follow the signs.

Bird Street
One of the hobbies, particularly of older Chinese men, is keeping singing birds. They will often gather in parks and open spaces to compare and show off their birds which are kept in small, often ornate but easily hung cages.

At Bird Street, which is very close to the end of Flower Market Street, up a short flight of steps, you will see all manner of birds for sale and the accessories which come with them.

You will hear the chirping and singing of the birds before you arrive and the variety of creatures available is truly amazing - everything from small finches to large parrots.

Aplui Street
This is an open air street market next to Sham Shu Po MTR station (Exit A) and it sells all manner of electronic gadgets, lights and electrical equipment. Some new and others second hand. Some of the shops which line the market specialize in computer accessories but be careful that you are buying genuine items and not clever imitations. In nearby streets are numerous bead shops for jewelry making enthusiasts, as well as several computer arcades.

The Jade Market
This is an interesting covered market in two sections at the junction of Battery Street and Kansu Street in Yau Ma Tei, quite close to Temple Street. As well as jade, you can also buy pearls and other gemstones.

There is also a wide selection of old Chinese artifacts and curios here. It helps to have some knowledge of jade as it comes in different levels of quality and color shades (not always green). Some of the vendors will make up necklaces for you. Many of the stalls sell similar pieces and it is worth comparing prices before buying.

Go to Yau Ma Tei MTR, exit at C and follow the tourist signs.

Where can I get a bargain?

When Hong Kong manufacturing was at its height in the fifties, sixties and seventies, Hong Kong was a shopper's paradise. Now that many of the factories have moved to the economically buoyant markets of China, Hong Kong has morphed into an international finance center and prices have escalated.

Hong Kong has become an increasingly expensive region in which to live. The 'Numbeo' Cost of Living Index which lists world cities in order of their expensiveness, according to rent, groceries, restaurants and local purchasing power places Hong Kong 60th out of the 497 represented. Singapore is the only Asian city which is more expensive. Rents and real estate are particularly costly in the territory, especially those within reach of the harbor.

Many retail commodities are cheaper in other parts of South East Asia. Having said this, Hong Kong is still a competitive place for some goods and here are a selection of them.

Made to measure suits
Hong Kong has a wealth of tailor shops, many owned by Indian families around the Nathan Road area of TST. You will soon be aware of this if you walk along the upper end of the road opposite Kowloon Park. If you look like a tourist, you will be repeatedly approached, handed name cards and asked – "Nice suit for you Sir? Nice jacket Madam?"

Many of the tailors will promise delivery within 24 hours. Like everything, the quality is variable and if you pay very low prices, you will probably get a less than perfect item. Tailors thrive on their reputation and, if you want some items made, look for written commendations and check reviews on tourist websites.

Certainly the most famous of the Hong Kong tailors is Sam's Tailor in Burlington Arcade at 90 Nathan Road. Sam and his family have made suits and shirts for some very famous politicians, royalty and show business personalities

and you can see photos of Sam alongside many of them. There are a large number of other reputable tailors including the long established Punjab House at 5/F Golden Crown Court, 60 Nathan Road, TST and Raja Fashions at 34C, Cameron Road TST.

Cameras
Hong Kong has a large number of camera shops – both new and second hand. It has a reputation for being one of the best places in the world for cameras and photographic accessories but with the development of online shopping giants, it is not necessarily the cheapest.

There is, however, no sales tax in Hong Kong and you can closely examine what you are buying. You should be aware that major camera brands will often not offer international warranties, and they are likely to be only be valid in Hong Kong. You may also have to pay an extra percentage in the smaller shops if you pay by credit card.

You should have a clear idea of what is a reasonable price before entering a shop and in the tourist areas you should be wary of display goods with no price tag.

Look out for the Hong Kong Tourism Board logo to ensure you will have some comeback if the goods are faulty.

One of the best areas for photographic equipment is Stanley Street in Central, where prices tags are displayed. Also Wing Shing Photo Supplies at 55 Sai Yeung Choi Street, Mong Kok has a good reputation. In Kimberley Road TST, there are some shops which deal in second hand cameras and if you are knowledgeable it is possible to get a bargain there.

Electronics

Hongkongers are very up to date with the latest technical equipment, to the degree where they will queue for hours to be amongst the first to get the latest edition smart phone when it first comes out.

As with cameras, electronic equipment may not be much cheaper than in your home country, but you will be able to get the latest models and very knowledgeable sales staff will be able to explain the details and answer your questions.

Sin Tat Plaza at 83 Argyle Street sells a wide range of smartphones at reasonable prices. You can also take phones there to get them repaired or unlocked. You will need to research to ensure the phones are not region locked and that bands can be connected to your local data network

Fortress and Broadway the local rival chains also specialize in electronic equipment and have a good local reputation and legitimate warranties and return policies. Their outlets are in all major shopping malls, often next door to each other!

There are several computer arcades, which also sell endless accessories and you can compare prices and look for bargains. These include the Wan Chai Computer Centre at 144 Hennessy Road, The Golden Computer Arcade at 146 Fuk Wa Street, Sham Shui Po and Star Computer City, 2nd Floor Star House, 3 Salisbury Road TST.

There are large, modern and very busy Apple stores in Festival Walk, Causeway Bay and IFC Malls where English speaking assistants can give you advice about Apple computers and iPhones and how you can ensure they are compatible with your local network.

Other bargains which can be found in Hong Kong include luggage, jewelry, and local Art and antiques. Whatever your interest, it is wise to use your common sense and compare prices in several shops before buying.

Sport

A supportive government, first class stadiums and excellent facilities, have ensured Hong Kong's status as an important venue for local and international sport.

The Hong Kong Rugby Sevens

Perhaps the biggest and most prestigious of the annual sporting events, which always attracts a worldwide audience, is the Hong Kong Rugby Sevens competition. This is held at the Hong Kong Stadium at So Kong Po in late March or early April.

It attracts the best Sevens teams from all the major rugby playing nations, and tickets for all three days of the weekend event sell out well in advance - at HK$1800 they are not cheap! Supporters come from around the globe, and nearby hotels are often fully booked.

Hong Kong Island takes on a carnival atmosphere as thousands of young and not so young supporters descend upon the stadium - particularly the South Stand - in all manner of fancy dress. Despite a large amount of alcohol being consumed, there is rarely any trouble at the event and partisan supporters from around the world heckle each other with good spirit.

The teams are seeded into four competitions: the shield, plate, bowl and cup. The standard of rugby is extremely high, and the cup is fought keenly between such giants as New Zealand, South Africa, Australia, England and the most frequent winners, Fiji. Twenty Six nations compete in front of sell-out crowds of 40,000 on each of the three days.

The Sevens has been an eagerly anticipated event for 40 years and enthusiasts book their flights and accommodation a year in advance.

So Kong Po stadium is about a 15-minute walk from exit B2 of Causeway Bay MTR station. You cannot fail to find it on a Sevens day, you just follow the signs or the outrageously dressed fans!

The Hong Kong Standard Chartered Marathon

This is a major marathon, half marathon, 10km and wheelchair annual road race, sponsored by the Standard Chartered Bank and it attracts elite athletes from all around the world.

The race is held on a Sunday in January or February when the weather is a little cooler, commencing very early in the morning. The route is very much an urban one, with some uphill sections.

The event is very popular and it usually attracts its maximum number of a staggering 70,000 competitors for all four races, and late applications are often unsuccessful.

It was first held as a cross border event in the handover year of 1997, but logistical difficulties were such that this only happened on the one occasion. Since then, the route has varied but is now mainly in urban parts of Kowloon and Hong Kong Island. It is considered a difficult marathon route because of the possibility of high humidity and some steep uphill sections.

The early start permits certain roads to be cordoned off, and it usually crosses the harbor through one of the road tunnels, which is temporarily closed to traffic. The winning time for the Men's event in 2016 was 2:12:12 for men and for women it was 2:36:51, with both athletes from East Africa.

The 10 km run attracts very large numbers which is disadvantageous at the start as, unless you are an elite runner who begins at the front, the crowds make it difficult to get into a running stride for several minutes.

The Hong Kong Open Golf Tournament

This event is held at Hong Kong Golf Club's exclusive Fanling course, in the North East New Territories, close to the border with China. It has been an annual event since 1959 and the competition usually takes place from Thursday until Sunday towards the end of November.

It is co-sanctioned by the Asian Tour and the European Tour and attracts world class competitors.

The winner of the 2015 competition was Justin Rose. Past winners have included Miguel Angel Jimenez (4 times), Rory McIlroy, Ian Poulter, Colin Montgomerie, Berhard Langer and Greg Norman.

The Hong Kong Golf Club organizes a free shuttle bus from nearby Sheung Shui MTR station on the East Rail line.

Golf in Hong Kong:
The sport has become increasingly popular in Hong Kong and there are several driving ranges in different locations.

There are also some very exclusive golf courses where membership is very expensive. There is one public golf complex on the island of Kai Sai Chau near Sai Kung. This is owned and run by the Hong Kong Jockey Club and includes 3 courses, club house, driving range, tuition and hire facilities.

It is necessary to book beforehand and the courses get very busy, especially at weekends. The dedicated golf course hover ferry runs frequently from the Sai Kung Waterfront.

Swimming

Hong Kong has well maintained and supervised public swimming pools scattered around the territory. The outdoor pools are open during the summer and the indoor pools are open throughout the year. Some are Olympic sized (50 meters), for example the Sai King Public Swimming Pool.

Entry is inexpensive - typically about HK$30 including the use of a locker for your belongings. Public pools do get very crowded during the summer months, especially at weekends. They are run by the government's Leisure and Cultural Services Department and their location and opening hours can be found by checking the Department's web site at www.lcsd.gov.hk/en.

There is annual cross harbor swimming race from East Kowloon to Quarry Bay where the distance across the harbor is about 1.5km. The event has an historical link. It was held annually from 1906 until it was suspended in 1979 when the water quality of the harbor was considered too polluted. After a clean-up of the harbor and a significant improvement in water quality, the race was reinstated in 2011.

Over 2000 elite swimmers from all over the region participate in the race, in various categories. The event takes place on a Sunday in October. The fastest time in 2015 was just over 13 minutes and 46 seconds.

Prudential Hong Kong Open Tennis Tournament

This event was re-introduced in 2014 at the hard courts of Victoria Park tennis arena in Causeway Bay and it is a Premier Women's International event sanctioned by the Women's Tennis Association.

The tournament takes place over one week (Saturday to Saturday) in mid-October. The Open attracts world class tennis players who compete for a share of the US$250,000 prize money.

Winners of the past two competitions were Jelena Jankovic in 2015 and Sabine Lisicki in 2014.

Dragon Boat Racing

Hong Kong is the home of dragon boat racing and even has a public holiday to celebrate the ancient sport.

As well as the local races in June, Hong Kong also hosts the International Dragon Boat championships, sponsored by Hong Kong Tourism Board and The Hong Kong China Dragon Boat Association.

This is a three day event held in Victoria harbor and there is a fantastic party atmosphere with stalls and entertainment to accompany the highly competitive races.

The Hong Kong Cyclophon

Cycling has become more and more popular in the territory and there are several dedicated bicycle paths with nearby bike rental shops. You will also see brightly attired racing cyclists on the New Territories roads, often in groups.

The Hong Kong Tourist Board, recognizing the increasing interest in the sport, organized the first Hong Kong Cyclophon in autumn 2015.

This attracted over 3,500 participants in different categories from 17 countries, including amateur and professional riders. There are numerous cycling clubs in the territory.

A state-of-the-art 250 meter velodrome was opened at Tsueng Kwan O Sports Ground in 2013. It has room for 3000 spectators.

Horse Racing

Horse racing is very popular in Hong Kong and the two world class courses (Happy Valley and Sha Tin) are always busy on race days (Wednesday evening, and either Saturday or Sunday afternoon).

At the weekend, there are usually ten races starting at 12:45 with 30 minutes between races for punters to select their choice/collect their winnings or bemoan their fate. There is a maximum of 14 horses in each race and they start from a purpose built starting gate. If you want a lesson in efficiency you should witness how well organized the races are with no time lost or wasted.

The floodlit Wednesday meetings are shorter (8 races) but particularly atmospheric, especially at Happy Valley, which has been in operation since 1846! To enter either of the race courses costs a mere HK$10 and you can watch the horses from quite close to the rail. The amount of money you might lose, of course, is another matter!

All of the betting is strictly overseen by the Hong Kong Jockey Club. Special races are held on January 1st and on the 3rd day of Chinese New Year. The latter is interspersed with dragon and lion dances.

The Longines HK International Races is arguably the highlight of the racing calendar and has been taking place in December each year since 1988. This is one of the most important fixtures for jockeys, trainers and owners worldwide. It is recognized as the 'Turf World Championship' and offers some very lucrative prizes. The total prize money was HK$83 million in 2015.

There are four trophies at different distances which are keenly fought, as well as the Longines International Jockey's championship, which is decided a few days before.

Ice Skating

There are several Ice Rinks in Hong Kong, usually in shopping malls. They offer skate hire as well as tuition.

Rinks can be found at Festival Walk in Kowloon Tong, Elements Shopping Mall in TST, Cityplaza in Tai Koo Shing, Mega Box in Kowloon Bay, the Dragon Centre in Sham Shui Po and at the Riviera Ice Chalet in Tseun Wan.

Football

Football is the most popular sport in Hong Kong and there are numerous teams who play at weekends throughout the territory. There are also three leagues with professional and semi-professional players.

The top league is the Hong Kong Premier League which has nine teams. There are several foreign players from such countries as Brazil, Spain, Ecuador and Korea who regularly play in the league but in order to encourage local players each team is limited to six players born outside the territory, only four of whom can be on the field at once.

Hong Kong has a national team which plays in the Asian Cup and the early stages of the World Cup. Its best performance was 3rd place in the Asian Cup in 1956. Hong Kong has never gone beyond the qualifying stages of the World Cup, but has had some commendable results in the competition. They are currently ranked at 143 in the FIFA rankings.

If you want to take in a Hong Kong Premier League game, many are played at either the Hong Kong Stadium or Mong Kok Stadium. The season runs from September until April. For fixtures check the Hong Kong Football Association website at www.hkfa.com/en.

There is a big following of the English Premier League (EPL) and several big clubs have been to the territory to play pre-season friendlies, including Manchester United, Manchester City, Liverpool and Sunderland.

There are Hong Kong branches of the major EPL supporters clubs and EPL games are shown live in many bars and pubs.

Cricket

The British legacy, as well as a significant South Asian population, has ensured that cricket is popular in the territory. There are over 30 cricket teams including two who are fully Chinese, which compete in the local Saturday and Sunday leagues. Hong Kong is ranked 15th in the world by the International Cricket Council.

Between 1992 and 2012 the annual Hong Kong Cricket Sixes took place in the territory and it attracted some of the best players in the world for a weekend in November.

The tournament lost its sponsor in 2012 but at the time of writing, talks are underway to reinstate the event. If it goes ahead the tournament will take place at The Kowloon Cricket Club in Coxes Road near Jordan MTR station.

Hong Kong Sports Institute

Hong Kong's easy access and its world class facilities have given it a high profile as a venue for less popular sports and International events are held in the territory for such sports as squash, judo, archery, water polo, ice hockey, figure skating, canoeing, rowing, sailing, gymnastics, fencing, netball, bowls and equestrian events.

In the 2008 Beijing Olympics all of the equestrian events took place at the Hong Kong Sports Institute (HKSI) adjacent to the Sha Tin racecourse, with the cooperation of the Hong Kong Jockey Club.

The HKSI runs an extensive program for elite sportsmen and women where funding and training support is given. This for both able bodied and disabled athletes.

Olympics and Paralympics

Hong Kong has sent teams to the Summer Olympic Games since 1952, the Winter Games since 2002 and the Paralympics since 1972. Before 1997 it competed under its own name but now it is known as 'Hong Kong China'. An agreement has been made with Beijing that in the event of a medal, the Hong Kong SAR Bauhinia flag would be raised but the national anthem played would be that of the People's Republic of China.

Hong Kong has won three Olympic medals. The greatest success was at Atlanta in 1996 when Cheung Chau windsurfer Lee Lai Shan won the gold in the Women's Sailboard (Mistrel) event. A silver medal was won for Hong Kong in Athens in 2004 at the men's doubles event by table tennis players Ko Lai Chan and Li Ching. In London in 2012 Lee Wai Sze won the bronze in the Women's Keirin cycling competition.

Hong Kong's performance in the Paralympics has been outstanding. It has won a total of 98 medals - 34 gold, 29 silver and 35 bronze. Hong Kong's first Paralympic gold medals were won in 1984.

In the 2016 Paralympics in Rio de Janeiro, Hong Kong competitors won gold medals for boccia and swimming, also two silvers and a bronze for wheelchair fencing and an additional bronze for table tennis.

Annual Events

Here is our month by month summary of a selection of Hong Kong's annual events, as well as the typical weather conditions. At the time of writing, not all event organizers have confirmed the exact start dates of these events - you should check the appropriate websites closer to the time.

January

January is Hong Kong's coldest month. The average temperature is 15°C (59°F) which although mild by the standards of many visitors, is cold enough for the locals to don extra layers of clothing.

Homes in Hong Kong are designed to keep the cold out and it can be a little more difficult to keep warm indoors during January. Your hotel will probably have a heater, as occasionally the temperature may drop at night to 4 or 5 degrees Celcius.

Snow is unheard of but there might be a rare appearance of frost on Tai Mo Shan, the highest point in the territory. It is the driest month with an average of 33mm of rainfall over just four days. The humidity is low and it is a good month for hiking and exploring the outside. You will still catch the Christmas lights in the first few days of the month and New Year's

Day is a public holiday.

January Events
New Year's Day Horse Racing meeting at either Sha Tin or Happy Valley with dragon and lion dances. New Year's Day is a Sunday in 2017, so Monday 2nd January will be a public holiday.

The special *Christmas events* at Disneyland and Ocean Park will run on for the first few days of the month.

Hong Kong Toys and Games Fair – Hong Kong Convention and Exhibition Centre. This is

the largest toy industry event in Asia and exhibits include branded toys, educational toys, electronic and remote controlled toys and party items. In 2017 this will take place from 9th to 12th.

Chinese New Year - The first new moon between the 21st January and 20th February (In 2017 this will be on January 28th). There will be lion and dragon dances, a parade and a fireworks display. The 28th, 29th and 30th are official public holidays.

February

The weather in February is much like January's with average temperatures of 15°C (59°F). It is less cold at night and it rarely falls below 10°C. The average rainfall is 45mm over five days and the humidity remains low.

The beginning of the month is centered around the Chinese New Year celebrations and you are sure to see lion and dragon dances. Many of the large skyscrapers are decorated with ornate lights depicting the themes of the animal whose year is being celebrated

The 2016/17 Year of the Monkey will be replaced by the Year of the Rooster and followed by the Dog and Pig. Then the twelve-year cycle begins again.

February Events
Continuing Chinese New Year celebrations – fireworks, parade, horse races, lion and dragon dances.

The Standard Chartered Marathon, Half Marathon and Ten Kilometer races. In 2017, this will be on the 12th.

Hong Kong Arts Festival begins. This is a four-week Festival featuring a much anticipated program of live performing arts in various venues all over the territory. It includes world famous orchestras, music performers, dancers and drama groups. In 2017 it

runs from 16th February to 18th March.

Longines Masters of Hong Kong Equestrian Event (AsiaWorld Expo). This is a combined Sport, Fashion and Art event with big names in equestrianism performing alongside social and lifestyle events. This will take place from 10th to 12th in 2017.

March

In March the weather begins to warm up with daily temperatures averaging 18°C (64°F) and rarely dipping below 15°C. The rainfall is twice that of January averaging 74mm with 7 days of rain and relatively low humidity.

March Events
The *Hong Kong Arts Festival* continues until the middle of the month.

Hong Kong Film Festival – This is a three-week festival of films from around the world. Venues include Hong Kong Convention and Exhibition Centre (HKCEC), Hong Kong Cultural Centre and City Hall. The dates for 2017 are March 21st to April 4th and the website is www.hkiff.org.hk

Hong Kong Flower Show – This flower show is held at Victoria Park. Dates have not yet been announced.

Hong Kong International Jewelry Show – March 2nd to 6th, 2017

Art Basel Hong Kong – This International Art Exhibition takes place at HKCEC from 23rd to 25th March in 2017.

April

April is a popular month for visiting Hong Kong. Although the humidity is a little higher, days are mainly sunny and the average temperature is 22°C (72°F). You might need an umbrella as rainfall averages 137mm with eight days of rain in the month. As the month reaches its end the humidity begins to rise sharply.

April Events
Ching Ming Festival. This is a public holiday in Hong Kong where local people will visit graves of their ancestors, burn paper money and other replicas and pay their respects. It is on April 4th in 2017. Areas around cemeteries will get very crowded.

The *Hong Kong Sevens* takes place at San Po Kong Stadium near Causeway Bay, this three day event is the highlight of many sports fans' year. There is a pre-Sevens carnival and parade at Lan Kwai Fong and a concert at 'The Sevens Village' near the stadium. In 2017 this event will be from April 7th to 9th.

Hong Kong Electronics Fair at HKCEC – Worldwide innovative products are showcased here. In 2017 this will be from 13th to 16th.

May

The average temperature in May is 25°C (77°F) but it often feels hotter because humidity levels rise sharply. May is quite a wet month with an average of 292mm and it can rain for fourteen or fifteen days. It also marks the beginning of the Typhoon season, although these are more likely to occur later in the summer.

May Events

Labor Day on May 1st is an official public holiday.

Cheung Chau bun festival – This is a week of parades, lion dances and a 'bun scrambling contest' on Cheung Chau Island. In 2017 this will be around May 3rd.

Buddha's Birthday –The date varies and it is an official public holiday; in 2017 it will be on May 3rd. There are rituals at monasteries, shrines and temples throughout the territory.

June

Summer arrives with a vengeance in June. Although the average temperature is 28°C (82.5°F), there can be days in the thirties with accompanying high humidity. You will need lots of changes of clothing if you do any walking outside. You will also need to drink a large amount of liquids to keep hydrated. There is usually a lot of rain in June with an average of 394mm falling on 18 days of the month.

June Events

Dragon Boat Festival (Tseng Ng) - There is a public holiday in the first half of the month to celebrate this and territory-wide dragon boat races are held. The largest venues for races are Sha Tin, Stanley, Sai Kung and Aberdeen. In 2017, Tseng Ng will unusually fall in May 30th.

International Dragon Boat Festival - This is a three-day event which occurs a few days later and includes accompanying entertainers, marching bands and lion dances.

Chinese Opera Festival - Stage performances of this unique form of entertainment are held in various locations throughout the territory including the HK Cultural Centre and City Hall near the Central waterfront.

Hong Kong Jewelry and Gem Fair - This June event is one of the top three of Asia's fine jewelry events. Over 2,300 exhibitors from 45 countries exhibit over four days at the HKCEC. In 2017 it takes place from June 22nd to 25th.

July

The average temperature in July is 30°C and the high humidity is ever present. If you are outdoors for any length of time you will need lots of changes of light clothing. Rainfall is still high and averages 381mm over 17 days and there is a possibility of a typhoon.

Events in July

Establishment of HKSAR day - This is a public holiday on July 1st which commemorates the handover of Hong Kong from the Britain to China on July 1st 1997. There will be flag raising ceremonies, parades and cultural performances.

International Arts Carnival - This is put together each year and includes such family entertainment as theatre, music, dance, film and magic. There are also outreach workshops and backstage tours.

Hong Kong Trade Development Council Book Fair, HKCEC - This is an exhibition of traditional books and also multimedia e-books and e-learning resources. There are also seminars and signing events with well-known authors. Books are also on sale. 2017 dates are July 19th to 25th.

August

The August weather is very similar to July's, with temperatures averaging 29°C and continuing high levels of humidity. On average 367mm of rain will fall on 15 days and you must be aware of the chance of thunderstorms and possible typhoons.

Many long term expatriates vacate the territory to return to their cooler home countries at some time during the traditional school holiday months of July and August.

Events in August

August is a relatively quiet month for events in Hong Kong, but there are three worth considering. They all take place at the HKCEC at various times during the month. Please check the HKCEC website for 2017 dates.

Ani-Com Games Exhibition - This is an exhibition of the latest digital entertainment, comics, video games, toys and related collectable.

Hong Kong Food Expo - This is a five-day event sponsored by the Hong Kong Trade Development Council and it attracts more than 900 exhibitors from around the world with their unique selections of food and delicacies. There are also cookery demonstrations, as well as forums on such topics as food nutrition and safety.

Hong Kong Computer and Communications Festival - This is organized by the Chamber of Hong Kong Computer Industry and is the largest exhibition of the IT industry in the territory. There are items for sale to the public and anyone interested in computers, gadgets or things digital will be well catered for.

September

September is still a hot month by any standards with average temperatures standing at 27°C, but the good news is that the long humid spell is beginning to abate. Rainfall is 257mm with an average of 12 rainy days and the chances of a typhoon are now slimmer.

September Events

Mid-Autumn (Lantern) Festival - This, like all of the traditional Chinese celebrations is governed by the lunar year, and it is on the eighth full moon in the Chinese lunar calendar which is usually in late September. Historically, families gathered beneath the full moon to eat mooncakes and celebrate the harvest. It is still very much a family event loved by lantern toting children.

There are several events associated with this and the day following Mid-Autumn Festival is a public holiday. In 2017, the event runs on October 4th to 6th, with the public holiday falling on October 5th.

Lantern display at Victoria Park - Thousands of lanterns are on display around a chosen design winning centerpiece.

Tsim Sha Tsi Thematic Lantern Exhibition - This is in the piazza outside the Hong Kong Cultural Centre near Star Ferry.

Tai Hang Fire Dragon Dance - This takes place on three consecutive nights when an immense (67m) fire dragon is paraded through the streets of Tai Hang (near Causeway Bay). Over 300 performers carry the dragon and it is accompanied by firecrackers and thousands of burning joss sticks. In 2016, the Dance will be from 14th to 16th.

The Hong Kong Watch and Clock Fair – This is the world's largest timepiece event and features numerous examples from around the world, as well as information about the latest designs and trends in the market. The dates for 2017 are 5th to 9th.

October

October is a good month weather-wise. The skies are often clear and blue and the temperature averages a pleasant 25°C. Beaches become busy and hiking is popular. The sun can be damaging, however, and you should take the usual precautions if you are going to be outside for any length of time. Rainfall averages 150mm over 8 days.

October Events

National Day is on October 1st. This is a public holiday but because it falls on a Sunday in 2017, the following day becomes a holiday. National Day commemorates the founding of the People's Republic of China in 1949.

There are various events around the territory connected with this including flag raising ceremonies and parades and a lavish firework display in Victoria Harbor. This usually starts at 9:00pm and lasts for about 20 minutes. Good views of the fireworks can be obtained all along the Central and TST waterfronts and from any of the high buildings with a harbor outlook.

Hong Kong International Jazz Festival - This is a well anticipated annual event that draws world class performers. Venues are the City Hall in Central and the Cultural Centre in TST, with free concerts in the latter's piazza.

Hong Kong Tennis Open (Ladies) – Held in Victoria Park. 2017 dates are to be confirmed.

Hong Kong Cyclophon – This took place for the first time in 2015 and the venue is subject to confirmation.

Chung Yeung Festival - This is a similar event to Ching Ming. It is a public holiday set aside for respecting ancestors. Areas around cemeteries and columbaria will be very busy. The official date in 2017 is the 28th.

Wine and Dine Festival - This annual event is held along the Central waterfront near the ferry piers. Over 300 booths celebrate wine and food from around the world. This three day event includes live entertainment, signature dishes, cookery demonstrations, food sampling and wine tasting. In 2016 it will be

held from 27th to 30th.

German October Bierfest - This is Asia's longest running German Beer festival and it takes place annually outdoors on the viewing platform of the Marco Polo Hotel at Harbor City TST, surrounded by stunning night harbor views. Thousands of visitors head for the specially erected marquee to eat authentic German food, clink beer steins and listen to 'oom pah pah' bands. Dates for 2017 are to be confirmed.

Halloween Celebrations - There are major events around the theme of Halloween at Disneyland and Ocean Park as well as an elaborate street party at Lan Kwai Fong on 31st October. If you attend you should consider arriving suitably dressed!

November

November is another very pleasant month as far as the weather is concerned with average temperatures of about 23°C and low rainfall (just 35mm over 5 days). the skies are often clear The temperature starts to dip a little towards the end of the month.

Events in November
Hong Kong International Wine and Spirits Fair - This is the largest wine show in Asia and features wines from nearly 40 regions of the world. This three day event takes place at the HKCEC and in 2016 it will be held from November 10th to 12th.

Hong Kong International Literary Festival - This annual event features emerging and established writers from around the world. The program includes discussions, literary lunches, workshops and book signings in various venues. 2016 dates are November 5th to 13th.

Symphony Under the Stars - This is an annual free outdoor concert by the prestigious Hong Kong Philharmonic Orchestra. It takes place at the Central Harborfront Event Space. Tickets are free but pre-registration is required. The event is on November 12th in 2016.

Lan Kwai Fong Carnival - On the cobbled streets of Lan Kwai Fong this is a weekend street party including a colorful parade, arts and crafts, African drummers, fortune tellers, magicians and live music. Street food and beer is on sale until the early hours.

Hong Kong Trailwalker – An Oxfam sponsored hike across the territory along the MacLehose Trail. In 2016, this will begin on Friday 18th.

December

Although the weather becomes cooler in December, it is generally dry and you are still likely to get clear skies and low humidity. The average temperature for the month is 20°C with 34mm of rain over just 5 days. It is usually excellent for hiking.

December Events
Christmas - Ornate Christmas trees appear in shopping malls and many of the skyscrapers which line the harbor have spectacular colored lights draped across them. You will be able to hear children's carol concerts at different venues around the territory and most of the big malls will have a resident Santa to greet the children.

The two major theme parks, Disneyland and Ocean Park put on special Christmas themed events from early December.

The *Hong Kong Open Golf Competition* takes place December 8th to 11th 2016.

The *Longines Hong Kong International Races* is on December 13th in 2016.

Lan Kai Fong Christmas and New Year Parties (December 24th and 31st) - The festive spirit is displayed in abundance in the famous nightlife area of Central with colorful decorations and street parties. They are well attended on both occasions.

New Year Countdown - A spectacular firework display, synchronized to rousing music takes place at midnight on December 31st. The vantage points along the waterfront on both sides of the harbor get busy and we recommend that you to arrive early.

1-Week Sample Itinerary

Most visitors come to Hong Kong for a shorter period of time, but there are more than enough activities to fill an entire week as you will see in this section.

For those who have less than a week, the 'must dos' include Star Ferry, the Peak, the Symphony of Lights Show, a visit to a temple and, of course, you should sample some of the famous, local cooking.

The following itinerary assumes that you want to get as much out of your visit as you can, you have plenty of energy and that you arrive during one of the less hot months.

If you complete it all, you will have had some good experiences, have a good idea of different aspects of Hong Kong and will be ready for a quieter holiday elsewhere!

Our suggestions are based on staying in TST and beginning the tour on a Monday.

Day One

Set off at 8:30 on Monday morning and cross Star Ferry and board the open top bus number 15C from near the Central Ferry Pier to the foot of the Peak Tram. Buy return tickets and take the Peak Tram to the summit.

You can then do the Peak Circle Walk which begins at Luard Road near the Peak Tower, and takes about an hour. Spend the rest of the morning taking photographs and browsing the shops on the Peak and have lunch at one of the restaurants.

Descend on the tram and cross Garden Road, following signs to the Hong Kong Botanical

and Zoological gardens. Spend an hour or two walking around the gardens and the animal exhibits.

Stroll down to Central via St John's Cathedral (look around inside) and Battery Path to Statue Square.

Take photos of the HSBC lions, the Bank of China and the old LegCo Building.

Catch a tram in Des

Voeux Road for the short ride to Western Market. Look around the market and browse the Chinese Medicine shops in nearby Wing Lok Street.

Catch the MTR from Sheung Wan station back to TST, changing at Admiralty.

Have dinner at one of the TST restaurants (maybe the Spring Deer if you have booked beforehand).

Day Two

On Tuesday, walk from your hotel along Chatham Road to the Science Museum, arriving soon after opening time at 10:00am. Spend two interesting and enjoyable hours especially in the children's gallery.

Cross by the footbridge to TST East for lunch.

Walk to Hung Hom MTR station and catch the East Rail line to Sha Tin. Follow signs

from the station and climb the steps to the Ten Thousand Buddhas Monastery and look around there for an hour.

On your return, walk through the New Town Plaza shopping mall and explore Sha Tin Park. Have dinner at one of the Sha Tin hotels (The Royal Park has an excellent buffet) or at a restaurant in the Plaza.

Catch MTR back to TST, changing at Kowloon Tong and Mong Kok.

Day Three

On Wednesday, catch the MTR for one stop to Admiralty. Leave at exit B and take the shuttle bus number 629 to Ocean Park.

You can spend all day there watching the various animal shows, observing the exhibits and riding the thrill rides.

At the lower exit, catch a taxi to Aberdeen Promenade and take the shuttle boat to the Jumbo Floating Restaurant for your evening meal (having booked beforehand).

Catch bus number 70 bus back to Central and return to TST by MTR.

Day Four

On Thursday, go by MTR to Tung Chung, changing trains at Lai King and follow signs to the cable car to go up to Ngong Ping. Buy a single ticket and take lots of photographs of the landscape below.

At the top, walk up the steps to see the Big Buddha, and look at the exhibition beneath it. Visit Po Lin Monastery and eat a Buddhist vegetarian lunch there.

Catch the Lantau Bus Number 2 to Mui Wo and spend an hour on the beach.

Return on the ferry to Central and have an early dinner in time to catch the Symphony of Light show at 8pm along the Central Waterfront.

Take Star Ferry back to TST, taking photos of the Hong Kong Nightscape.

Day Five

On Friday, after crossing the harbor on Star Ferry walk along the elevated footway to HSBC in Central turn right into Queens Road and walk for 10 minutes to the Mid-Levels escalator on your left.

Ascend the escalator as far as Hollywood Road and turn right following Cat Street signs into Upper Lascar Street.

Browse Cat Street's antiques and curios.

Walk up nearby Ladder Street (which is steep and narrow) as far as Caine Road and on your right you will find the Museum of Medical Science. You can spend an interesting hour here.

Walk down Tank Lane, which is next to the museum, and keep heading downhill until you come to Queen's Road. Turn to your left and you will soon reach Sheung Wan MTR station.

Return to Central by MTR and take Exit A for Exchange Square bus station.

Catch the 6X bus to Stanley Market. Spend an hour or two at the market and visit the Tin Hau temple to read about the aged tiger skin on the wall.

Eat at one of the restaurants in the relocated Murray House, catch the 6X bus back to Central and take the MTR to TST.

Day Six

On Saturday, walk along Chatham Road to The Hong Kong Museum of History for opening time at 10:00am and spend two hours there.

Stroll back along the TST waterfront – looking at the Avenue of the Stars (if it is open) and cross by the Space Museum to Nathan Road.

Take the MTR at TST to Kowloon Tong (change at Mong Kok) and change to the West Rail as far as Tai Po Market. Visit the Railway Museum there.

After the museum, catch the 64K bus towards Yuen Long, and alight at Kam Tin.

Visit the Kat Tin Wai walled village on your left, wander the narrow streets and take some photos of the elderly ladies in their hats.

Catch the 64K bus again onward to Yuen Long Town Center and take the Light Rail Transit to Tuen Mun MTR station. Take the MTR West Rail all the way back to TST East. Walk along the underpass to TST station and exit at B1 to Kimberley Road Knutsford Terrace for your evening meal.

For an alternate afternoon if the weather

is fine, after your lunch take MTR from TST and change at Admiralty to Shau Kei Wan. Walk the Dragon's Back and have a swim at the beach at Shek O or Big Wave Bay.

Get bus number 9 back to Shau Kei Wan and take the MTR to Quarry Bay and eat in one of the restaurants in Cityplaza. Return to TST by MTR.

Day Seven

On Sunday, get up early and wander into Kowloon Park to watch the locals at their Tai Chi and early morning exercise.

Catch the MTR to Prince Edward and follow the signs for the Flower Market and at the end of Flower Market Street walk up the steps into Bird Street.

Take a taxi to Festival Walk in Kowloon Tong and have lunch there.

After lunch, catch the MTR on the Kwun Tong line just two stops to Wong Tai Sin and spend an hour at the temple.

Back on the MTR to Mong Kok and walk the length of the Ladies Market along Tung Choi Street to where it ends in Dundas Street. Turn right into Dundas Street and left into Nathan Road and walk as far as Yau Ma Tei MTR station.

Use the MTR subway to cross busy Nathan Road and come out at Exit near Temple Street.

In Temple Street, stop for noodles at a *dai pai dong* and then wander the length of the market taking in the fortune tellers and the Cantonese Opera.

At the end of Temple Street turn left into Jordan Road and cross Nathan Road ahead of you.

Take bus number 1, 2 or 9 along the 'Golden Mile' back to TST. Return to your hotel for a well-deserved rest!

Further Reading

If you would like to learn more about Hong Kong, there are some superb books, both fiction and non-fiction which are set in the territory. They will give you a good historical background and help your understanding of why Hong Kong is the success story it is. Below are short summaries of our top five Hong Kong books in no particular order; there are many others.

1. Gweilo by Martin Booth - An account of being white and growing up in Hong Kong.

2. Diamond Hill by Feng Chi-shun - This book describes life in one of the poorest parts of Hong Kong.

3. Ghetto at the Center of the World by Gordon Mathews - A compelling study by a local academic and anthropologist of the infamous Chungking Mansions - which is a dilapidated seventeen floor building in the tourist district. Mathews looks at some of the individual success stories and attempts to make some sense of the complex inter-relationships.

4. Chasing the Dragon by Jackie Pullinger - An account of living in the notorious Kowloon Walled City working with drug addicts before its demolition in 1994.

5. Noble House by James Clavell - An epic book of over 1000 pages with numerous interweaving story lines. The book tells of the plotting and intrigue surrounding a British Hong Kong Trading Company (Struan's) in the backdrop of the impending Vietnam War.

A Special Thanks

If you have made it this far, thank you very much for reading everything. We hope this guide will make a big difference to your trip to Hong Kong! Remember to take this guide with you while you are visiting this amazing place.

If you have any questions or wish to contact us, you can do so at www. independentguidebooks.com/contact-us/. If you have any corrections, feedback about any element of the guide, or a review of an attraction, hotel, area or restaurant – send us a message and we will get back to you.

We also encourage you to leave a review on the Amazon website, or wherever you have purchased this guide from. Your reviews make a huge difference in helping other people find this guide, and we really appreciate your help.

If you have enjoyed this guide, other travel guides in this series include:

• The Independent Guide to New York City
• The Independent Guide to Paris
• The Independent Guide to London
• The Independent Guide to Dubai
• The Independent Guide to Universal Orlando
• The Independent Guide to Disneyland
• The Independent Guide to Disneyland Paris
• The Independent Guide to Walt Disney World
• The Independent Guide to Universal Studios Hollywood

Have a fantastic time in Hong Kong!

Photo Credits:

Hong Kong Street (Intro) - MojoBaron; Map on page 6 - OpenStreetMap; Opium Smokers - fry_theonly; Old Flag - mroach; Typhoon aftermath (boat) - wunderground.com; Chris Price - Bridge in History section; HKJC - Je T.; LEGO Complex - Tksteven; HSBC Lion - Soham Banerjee; Tin Hau Temple - iris; Christmas lights - np@djjewell; Lai See Envelopes - Billibala; Dragon Boat Races - southlooopliving; Cathay Pacific pane - Michael Rehfeldt; Traffic - Gunnar Grimnes; Octopus Card - Pawel Loj; Double Decker Bus - Hans-johnson; MTR - Michael E Lee; Tram - Eduardo M. C.; Night Star Ferry large - Nate Robert; Skyline large - Mike Behnken; The Star Ferry - Faungg; Peak Tram and Rugby Sevens - Jon Parise; Big Buddha - Ms. Anthea; Sky 100 - Barbara Willi; Symphony of Lights - Nik Cyclist; Avenue of the Stars - Edwin Lee; Ocean Park - Martin Lewison; HK Disneyland - Jeremy Thompson; Museum of History - brownpau; Space Museum - Julien Gong Min; Coastal Defence Museum - beeyourguide.com; Hong Kong Railway Museum - Chriskay; Heritage Museum - Thanate Tan; Nan Lian Garden - Gavin Anderson; Sha Tin Park - Sjors Provoost; Mid-levels escalator - Doug Letterman; Noon Day Gun Salute - Ozzy Delaney; Trail Sign and Marathon - David Woo; San Kung Fish Tank Restaurant - Denise Chan; Tai Po Kau - Ryan Fung; Stilt Houses - Jon Connell; Cheung Chau Boats - Tommy Wong; Hong Kong Beach - Luca Mascaro; Wetland Park - Byte Rider; Chopsticks - Rebecca Selah; MTR Cross Border - Galio; Peninsula Hotel - Chris Price; Kowloon Park - Cristian Bortes; Science museum - karendotcom127; Wong Tai Sin Temple - Daniel E Lee; Zoological and Botanical Gardens - Jason Cartwright; Jumbo restaurant - Arthur Chapman; Golden Bauhinia Square - wiredtourist.com; Temple of Ten Thousand Buddhas - Bernard Spragg; The Wilson Trail and Dragon Boats - Mark Lehmkuhler; Dragon's Back Trail - Rick McCharles; Boat Lunch - 'yosomono'; Hyatt Regency Interior - PYONKO; Burberyy Shopfront - Henry Lawford; Temple Street Fortune Tellers - IK's World Trip; Kate Moss - Sam's Tailor; Horse Racing - Tom Page; Football - See-ming Lee; Chinese New Year - Shankar S.; Equestrian - Craig Maccubbin;

COVER - Boat (Nicolas Vollmer), Skyline at night - Isaac Torrontera; Double Decker Tram, Boats, Flags and Vendors - Bernard Spragg; Temple Roof - Jaafar Alnasser Photography;

Maps adapted from WikiCommons illustrations.

15987430R10071

Printed in Poland
by Amazon Fulfillment
Poland Sp. z o.o., Wrocław